Country Roads
~ of ~
PENNSYLVANIA

*A Guide Book
from Country Roads Press*

Country Roads
~ of ~
PENNSYLVANIA

Sally Moore

Illustrated by
Janet Mecca

Country Roads Press
CASTINE · MAINE

Country Roads of Pennsylvania

Published by Country Roads Press
P.O. Box 286, Lower Main Street
Castine, Maine 04421

Text and cover design by Edith Allard.
Illustrations by Janet Mecca.

Library of Congress Cataloging-in-Publication Data
Moore, Sally, 1936–
    Country Roads of Pennsylvania /Sally Moore :
illustrated by Janet Mecca.
        p. cm.
    Includes index.
    ISBN 1-56626-032-9 : $9.95
    1. Pennsylvania—Guidebooks.   2. Automobile travel—
Pennsylvania—Guidebooks.   I. Title.
F147.3.M665   1993
917.4804'43—dc20   93-11611
                                                    CIP

Printed in the United States of America.
10   9   8   7   6   5   4   3   2

To Dick,
Sara-Lynn, Thom, and Karen

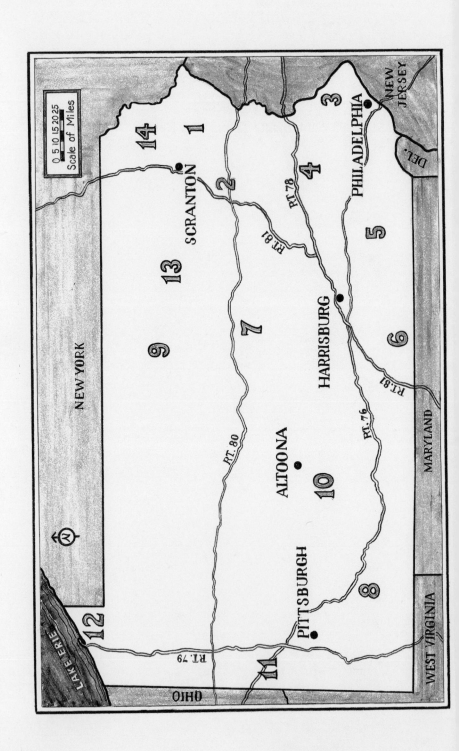

Contents

(& Key to Pennsylvania Country Roads)

Acknowledgments

I'd like to thank the people of the state of Pennsylvania for making me one of their own and for sharing their secrets with me. It would be impossible for me to enumerate all those who have been so generous with their time and knowledge, but in particular I'd like to express my gratitude to the many state and local tourism officials who work long and hard and who rendered invaluable assistance. Special verbal bouquets to Mark Hoy, director of the Pennsylvania Bureau of Travel Marketing; Lynn Neuman, his public relations assistant; and Terry Garvie, Pennsylvania Department of Transportation, who helped me untangle our byzantine system of road signing.

Introduction

The road less taken is a siren call to those of us whose lives are proscribed by a daily round of work and obligations. The desire to break away, to discover a new direction, a fresh compass heading, is a chance to reawaken the explorer in all of us. We can't chart the Northwest Passage as did Lewis and Clark or hunt for the Seven Golden Cities of Cíbola, but we can bypass the interstates and venture up that back-country road.

With more miles of state-maintained highway than New York and the New England states combined, Pennsylvania provides a splendid opportunity to discover out-of-the-way places. You can go antiquing, descend beneath the surface of the earth in a coal mine, dip your toes into one of the Great Lakes, or watch hawks and eagles as they soar on thermals over fall-flamed mountains. You can discover an elegant inn or hole up in a secluded bed and breakfast; you can dine on haute cuisine or belly up to the counter in an old-fashioned diner. There are wilderness trails to hike and wide Victorian porches to laze away a summer afternoon.

This guide has been researched and written to give you an idea of the many alternatives available throughout the Commonwealth during every season of the year. Each chapter opens with a routing and a description of area highlights. In making a selection of roads to follow and stopping points along the way, we haven't attempted comprehensive coverage. The choices are selective, aimed at giving the reader a sample of the many elements of geography, history, religious legacy, and heritage that define Pennsylvania's singular appeal.

It's a surprisingly diverse state, especially to visitors accustomed to thinking in terms of the large cities—Philadelphia and Pittsburgh—or along the lines of the rural coal country. Pennsylvania's 45,333 square miles encompass almost every geographical feature except desert and ocean. Mountains divide the land into three regions. The Appalachian Plateau, which runs from Wayne County in the northeast to Somerset County in the southwest, is a place of high, flat-topped divides riven by stream-etched valleys. To the east and south of the plateau country, long, narrow mountain ridges and valleys make up the Appalachian Mountain section. Southeast of the mountains lies the Great Valley, running diagonally from Northampton to Franklin counties.

There's a lot of territory for the back-country scout to explore, something canny Pennsylvanians discovered a long time ago. Ask anyone and they'll tell you about small villages where the residents have roots going back generations, not years, and about the country store carrying liniment and horse collars, not Martha Stewart collectibles. They'll mention the fifty-five state parks, where you don't have to arrive at dawn to get a picnic spot or brush elbows with a caravan of people on the hiking trails. And they'll give you tips on where to eat, because Pennsylvanians always travel on their stomachs. The place probably won't be fancy, but the coffee will be fresh and the pie homemade.

Before setting out on your journeys, you should be aware of a few idiosyncrasies endemic to back roads travel. Life proceeds at a slower pace. Avoid disappointment by planning as far in advance as possible. Many small inns and bed and breakfasts have a finite number of rooms, and if there's a big festival, a graduation at a nearby college, or the wedding of the chatelaine's daughter, the town may be booked solid. In addition, business hours for everything from museums to restaurants are very flexible; they change with the seasons and sometimes with owners' whims. For the sake of your sanity, call ahead.

The Pennsylvania Department of Transportation takes its cue for the state's route numbering system from the interstates. Most even-numbered highways run east and west; those ending in odd numbers run north and south. But don't look for iron-clad consistency, because there are numerous exceptions to the rule.

All routes are marked approximately every half mile with ten-inch by ten-inch or ten-inch by eighteen-inch white "segment markers," carrying the letters "SR" and the route number in two- to four-digit figures. Beneath the route designation is the segment number, which on north-south highways begins in the south, and on east-west highways begins in the west.

Explorers of old carried a map and compass; for today's country roads pioneers, a state highway map is a necessity, and an inexpensive dash-mounted compass a useful extra. A map and free travel guide listing special events, accommodations, regional contacts, welcome centers, ski areas, and more are available through the state travel office by calling 1 (800) VISIT PA.

To simplify road designations, I've used the following abbreviations: I = Interstate; US = U.S. Route or Highway; State = State Route or Highway.

Finally, remember that the voyage is as important as the destination, and every journey is formed by the character of the traveler. Take time to savor the experience, learn from the people you meet along the way, and enjoy your adventures on Pennsylvania's country roads.

1 ~

Pocono Retreat

Getting there: From Columbia, New Jersey, take I-80 into Pennsylvania to State 611.

Highlights: *For a weekend's journey, visit the Delaware Water Gap National Recreation Area, Dingman's Falls, one of the last privately owned toll bridges in the United States, Gifford Pinchot's Grey Towers, the Zane Grey Museum, the Roebling Aqueduct, the Dorflinger Glass Museum, the Stourbridge Lion, and craft and antique shops.*

The Route

From I-80 at Columbia, New Jersey, cross the bridge into Pennsylvania and connect with State 611 north to the town of Delaware Water Gap. Take the River Road, SR 2028, north to its terminus at US 209. Follow US 209 north to US 6 west at Milford, then State 434 and State 590 west to Hawley. There you rejoin US 6 west to Honesdale, a little town about twenty miles northeast of Scranton. The approximate total miles is seventy-one.

1

Like the folds and ridges of a pippin apple dried in the sun, the ancient Appalachians stretch through Pennsylvania from southwest to northeast. A part of this venerable chain, the Poconos are a 1,500-square-mile area of wooded uplands, rushing streams, and mirrored lakes. Divided by the Allegheny Front into the high uplands of the Pocono Plateau and the lower foothills, the region has been a mecca for travelers since the early 1800s, when wealthy Philadelphia Quaker families discovered respite from the city's summer heat and humidity in the cooler elevations of these northern hills.

Your gateway is the Columbia-Portland Bridge, which spans the Delaware from New Jersey to Pennsylvania. After a few miles of commercial clutter, the road changes abruptly as it matches course with the stream banked in summer by ripening blackberries and lush vegetation.

As you enter the Delaware Water Gap National Recreation Area, turn off State 611 at the sign for Slateford Farm and walk the grassy path back into the year 1790, when Washington was president and Samuel Pipher brought his family to farm this valley tract. Although this area is primarily agricultural, nearby outcroppings of slate fostered a local industry, and in 1868 the farm was purchased by a mining company, which boarded men in the farmhouse and cabin. On selected summer days, costumed rangers lead tours of the farm and interpret the early slate industry.

As you leave National Park Drive and return to State 611, you enter the Water Gap, a distinctive gorge where the Delaware River breaks through Blue, or Kittatinny, Mountain. Parking at Point of Gap overlook, turn to Mount Minsi at your back and compare its character to Mount Tammany across the river. They are two halves of the same mountain, scoured through by the abrasive action of water-driven sand and cobbles. Carefully cross the highway and railroad tracks, and find one of the fishermen's paths to the shore. Mount Tammany rises steeply from the river to 1,600 feet; downstream,

Browse through shops in Delware Water Gap

Canada geese honk and splash in the shallows of Arrow Island. Here and there along the shoreline, anglers lure smallmouth bass, muskies, or walleye.

Less than a mile upstream, the hamlet of Delaware Water Gap clings to the side of a hill. Founded in 1798 by Antoine Dutot, who built a trail from his sawmill in the Gap to the settlement, the town has a small weekend museum in the old village schoolhouse. A group of antique shops occupies what originally accommodated stores serving community needs. At the traffic light at the north end of town, the Village Farmer and Bakery turns out apple pie that puts mom's to shame.

To access the River Road, take care to avoid US 209, and bear right past the state information center. This is an excellent place to stop, orient yourself, and pick up the maps and brochures so generously provided.

The River Road is a roller coaster ride through a canopy of deciduous forests and thickets of rhododendron and laurel. Skirting the large resort complex of Shawnee, built on a great flat near the Delaware River, you pass through the quiet village, home to the Shawnee Theatre Summer Playhouse.

Beyond Shawnee, the road becomes even more winding as it passes Smithfield Beach, where you'll find a grassy picnic area and a sandy beach with bathhouses and lifeguards. Before joining US 209 at Bushkill, you go by park headquarters. Stop and learn what special programs the rangers have planned for the duration of your visit. You may learn about the Lenape, the original inhabitants of the area, or hear the hair-raising tale of the great Shohola train wreck, one of the worst in U.S. history. If you have a hankering to get out in the river to tube, canoe, or raft, pick up a list of local establishments renting river-worthy craft.

River Road ends at Fernwood, another huge resort that seems a town unto itself, with its condos, golf course, stables, and multisectioned inn. Head north, and stop at the crossroads of Bushkill Road and US 209. Abby's General Store is an old-fashioned, sell-everything emporium, where you can stop for a cold soda, a loaf of bread, or the latest gossip.

Across the road, the Pennsylvania Crafts Gallery specializes in top-quality work of artists from all around the state. Room after room of the old historic building is filled with jugs, jewelry, soft sculpture, and stained glass. This is the place to buy that special gift of Pennsylvania redware or a rainbow designer quilt.

You are now in the section of the park that is closed to commercial vehicles. Once a busy north-south route with heavy truck traffic, US 209 is now bucolic and stately, with the wide fields of the river bottomland to the east and high ridges of shale and sandstone to the west.

Dingmans Ferry was originally named Dingman's Choice after Andrew Dingman, a pioneer who operated a ferry across the river from 1735 to 1836. After the construction of several bridges and their destruction by natural forces, the current iron structure was completed in 1900. Operating under the original 1834 charter of the Dingman's Choice and Delaware Bridge Company, the third and present bridge on State 739 links Pennsylvania and New Jersey. As one of the last remaining privately owned toll bridges in the country, it is worth a short detour to see the white frame tollhouse bracketed in geraniums and chat with the structure's amicable attendants.

Located .8 mile west of US 209, Dingman's Falls is a blissfully noncommercial site: no candy stores or hot dog stands, just a visitors center staffed by the park service, and a small picnic area. A half-mile nature trail threads through thickets of rhododendron and towering hemlocks to two waterfalls. It tends to be a bit cool and wet under the trees, but the hike is worth the effort to see the waters of Dingman's Creek form delicate Silver Thread Falls or the cascades of Dingman's Falls.

Approaching Milford, the shale palisades rise to new heights. Beyond them and accessible by town roads is the Cliff Park Inn, a rambling white frame country inn with wraparound porches and panoramic views of the well-manicured nine-hole golf course. Operated by the Buchanan family since 1820, the inn has the mellow ambience of established tradition and an especially fine kitchen presided over by Graham Watson, chef de cuisine for fifteen years.

Milford is home to Grey Towers, the country estate of Gifford Pinchot, two-term governor of Pennsylvania and head of the U.S. Forest Service under President Theodore Roosevelt. A dedicated advocate of environmental conservation, Pinchot spent all his summers at the French chateau-esque home designed in 1885 for his father, James, by the renowned architect Richard Morris Hunt. When the forester turned to politics, he made Grey Towers his legal residence and married Cornelia Bryce, who transformed the mansion into a home more in keeping with the period.

The Forest Service now administers and maintains Grey Towers, and during the season provides tours of the house and formal gardens. A walk with a forester guide uncovers unexpected delights, such as the Bait Box, an elegant child's playhouse; the inky Reflecting Pool, a slash of mirrored water through the formal gardens; or the Fingerbowl, an outdoor dining area designed by Cornelia Pinchot. This raised pool edged in slate served as a circular counter where guests enjoyed the arbored shade and entertained themselves by passing food in floating wooden vessels.

Another remnant of Milford's past is the Upper Mill at the junction of 7th and Mill streets. One of six mills on this stretch of Van Tine Creek, this gristmill, with its twenty-four-foot waterwheel, dates to 1882 and ground commercial feed until the 1950s. Shops and boutiques have been built around the old works, providing an opportunity to shop while soaking up local history. Grab a bite of lunch at The Water Wheel Cafe and Bakery, where you can watch the laborious turn of the great wheel and enjoy gourmet sandwiches made with fresh-baked yeast breads.

In downtown Milford, the small Museum of the Pike County Historical Society showcases the area with a collection of artifacts donated by local citizens. "The Columns" has two bona fide claims to fame: a room dedicated to county resident Charles Sanders Peirce, mathematician, scientist, and founder of pragmatism, and the blood-stained American flag that cushioned Lincoln's head after his assassination at Ford's Theatre in Washington. Museum hours are quirky, so call first.

From Milford, US 6 winds through some of the Pocono's more pristine countryside. Leaving the Grand Army of the Republic Highway at State 434, leading to State 590, the road bends and curves to the Delaware River and the sleepy town of Lackawaxen. In 1905 the man noted as the "Father of the Western Novel" fled to this bucolic hamlet after an unsatisfy-ing life as a New York dentist. Zane Grey had often visited his brother Romer here to fish and relax, and it was here that he met his future wife, Dolly. After Grey's seven-year struggle as an author with only limited success, his most popular novel, *Riders of the Purple Sage,* was published, and he was on his way to fame and fortune. Called "the most popular author of the twentieth century," Grey wrote 89 books and numerous magazine articles and serials. Hollywood made 104 motion pictures from his novels.

Grey moved to California in 1918, but he never parted with the white frame house he purchased from his brother in 1914. After Grey's death, his widow sold the home to Helen James, daughter of a lifelong friend of Zane's, who operated it first as an inn and later as a museum. In 1989 the National Park Service purchased the house and collection and made extensive repairs and renovations. Today you can visit three rooms on the first floor, including the nook where Grey sat in his Morris chair composing his well-loved epics. The eclectic collection of Grey memorabilia includes items as diverse as his dentist's chair and mementos and trophies garnered as a skilled outdoorsman. An expert fisherman, Grey held ten world records, several of which stand today.

A short walk downstream from the museum is the Roebling Aqueduct, a forerunner of the Brooklyn Bridge, which Roebling and his son were to build in the 1880s. This oldest wire suspension bridge in the country was constructed by the Delaware & Hudson Canal Company, which transported its coal barges 109 miles from Honesdale to Rondout on the Hudson River near Kingston, New York. Where the canal boats crossed the Delaware with the aid of a rope ferry they often ran amuck of timber rafts, and canal company directors hired Roebling to engineer an aqueduct lifting the canal above the river. Today the aqueduct has been repaired and retrofitted for car traffic.

Leaving the river and continuing west to join US 6, you follow the remnants of the old canal to Hawley, once the railhead of the Pennsylvania Coal Company's Gravity Railroad. At Hawley, coal was transferred to the barges of the Delaware & Hudson Canal Company for the journey east. Present-day Hawley is a pleasant town of small shops, including the Woodloch Pines bakeshop in the old Watts Building at River and Main. If time constraints prevent you taking the short trek northeast of town to what many justifiably call the finest resort in the Poconos, you can at least munch one of the bakery's delicious muffins or pick up a jar of yummy strawberry preserves.

The Settlers Inn is another recommended hostelry. The gabled Tudor manor was built in 1927 by the community after the construction of Lake Wallenpaupack. Currently owned by Jean and Grant Genzlinger and Marsha Dunsmore, the inn has cozy rooms in the country style, a snug lounge, and a welcoming lobby where a fire burns on chilly days. Grant heads the extremely popular dining room (call for reservations, especially on weekends), and Marsha bakes all the breads, muffins, and pastries. A dinner specialty is roast duck—an outstanding rendition with crisp, flavorful skin and moist, tender flesh. The kitchen goes to great lengths to secure local Pennsylvania products for the table, and a formal herb garden is well tended for the fresh seasoning it provides.

Leaving Hawley and venturing north, you come to White Mills, scene of a thriving glass industry in the mid-1800s. The Dorflinger Glass Museum at the Dorflinger-Suydam Wildlife Sanctuary, about three-quarters of a mile from the town center, contains more than 600 pieces of glass that was considered elegant and beautiful enough for the tables of presidents from Lincoln to Wilson. This museum is a must-see for anyone who loves beautiful glass—antique or modern. There are examples of cut, engraved, etched, gilded, enameled, and colored crystal, and on sunny days the jeweled baubles displayed on window-mounted glass shelves throw diamond prisms all around.

The 600-acre wildlife sanctuary is graced with gardens, two lakes, and seven nature trails ranging from .35 mile to 1.4 miles. Summer art shows and a concert series are part of the yearly cycle of special events. The museum gift shop stocks a selection of glass gifts and collectibles and a comprehensive selection of books about glass.

Shortly before US 6 dips to the southwest and heads toward Scranton, Honesdale is located at what was the terminus of the Delaware & Hudson Canal. Once the largest coal market in the world, the small city now claims its fame as home of the Stourbridge Lion, the first steam locomotive to run in America. The locomotive, named for the fierce lion painted on the front of the boiler, was constructed in England and purchased by the canal company in the hope that it would prove more efficient at hauling coal than the Gravity Railroad. The plan was discarded after one trial run on August 29, 1829, when it was discovered that the locomotive was too heavy for the track. The original is in the Smithsonian, but a passenger car from the Gravity Railroad and a Lion replica built for the World's Fair of 1939 rest in a special pavilion on Main Street next to the Wayne County Historical Society Museum.

The museum is in a beautiful brick building that once housed the main offices of the canal company. Exhibits in the main galleries are exceptionally well displayed and feature glass from the many works that dotted the area at the time of the Dorflingers; artifacts and memorabilia from the D. & H. Canal Company and the Gravity Railroad; and paintings and etchings by local artists, including Jennie Brownscomb, who painted "The First Thanksgiving." The basement of the museum houses a collection of toys, kitchenware, tools, Indian artifacts, old musical instruments, and military paraphernalia from the Revolutionary through the Civil wars.

If you're in town weekends from June through Labor Day, you can relive the great age of railroads on a trip aboard the Stourbridge Line Rail Excursion. You board covered cars powered by one of only three BL-2 diesel engines still in operation for a round trip to Hawley or Lackawaxen, with an hour and a half stopover for shopping or sight-seeing. The ride takes you along the banks of the Lackawaxen River and past the stoneworks of the old canal. The conductors, brakemen, and engineers are volunteers, who communicate their love of the old rolling stock and enjoy telling people about the history and sights.

In the Area

All numbers are within area code 717.

Village Farmer and Bakery, Delaware Water Gap, 476-9440.

Delaware Water Gap National Recreation Area, park headquarters, Bushkill, 588-2451. Monday through Friday.

Abby's General Store, Bushkill, 588-6617. Daily.

Pennsylvania Crafts Gallery, Bushkill, 588-9156. Mid-May through the end of December. Hours vary.

Dingman's Falls Visitor Center, Dingman's Falls, 828-7802. May 1 through the end of October.

Cliff Park Inn & Golf Course, Milford, 296-6491 or 800-225-6535.

Grey Towers National Historic Landmark, Milford, 296-6401. Daily from 10:00 A.M. to 4:00 P.M. from Memorial Day weekend through Labor Day weekend; 1:00 P.M. to 4:00 P.M. daily from Labor Day through Veterans Day weekend.

The Upper Mill Waterwheel Cafe & Bakery, Milford, 296-2383.

The Columns, Milford, 296-8126. Hours vary.

Zane Grey Museum and Roebling Aqueduct, Lackawaxen, 685-4871. Daily from Memorial Day through Labor Day; weekends in April, May, September, and October.

Settlers Inn, Hawley, 226-2993 or 800-833-8527.

Woodloch Pines, Lake Teedyuskung, Hawley, 685-7121.

Woodloch Pines Bakery, Hawley, 226-1311.

The Dorflinger-Suydam Wildlife Sanctuary and Glass Museum, White Mills, Wednesday through Sunday from mid-May to November 1. 253-1185.

Wayne County Historical Society, Honesdale, 253-3240.
  Monday through Saturday from April through
  December; Tuesday, Thursday, and Saturday from
  January through March; Sunday afternoons in summer.

Stourbridge Line Rail Excursion, Honesdale, 253-1960.
  Weekends from June through Labor Day.

Pocono Mountains Vacation Bureau, Stroudsburg, 424-6050
  or 800-POCONOS.

2 ~

Anthracite Heritage

Getting there: Take I-81 to Scranton.

Highlights: *On a two- or three-day excursion into Pennsylvania's coal country, follow the tracks of the anthracite miner as you ride deep into the ground in actual mines in Scranton and Ashland. Learn the traditions and day-to-day existence of the hard-working immigrants who populated these northeastern regions, and visit Eckley, a "coal patch" town. Relive the glory days of American railroading at Steamtown National Historic Site.*

The Route

From I-81, take exit 57, the Carbondale/North Scranton Expressway, into the city. Leaving Scranton, again pick up I-81 at exit 53, the Scranton Expressway, and follow it south to exit 42, Dorrance. Stay on State 309 south to North Hazleton, and go east on State 940 to the outskirts of Jeddo, where you pick up SR 2051 east to Eckley.

Leaving the coal patch town, rejoin SR 2051 east to SR 3051 east and SR 4012 south to SR 4010 in Weatherly. Follow SR 4010 west, State 93 south, and US 209 east to Jim Thorpe.

13

From Jim Thorpe, take US 209 west and State 54 west to Ashland and Centralia. Pick up State 42 north to I-80, exit 34, Bloomsburg. The approximate total miles is 110.

Today's anthracite towns bear little resemblance to the gritty industrial hubs of the last century, when northeastern Pennsylvania became the supplier of 80 percent of the nation's coal. "King Coal" no longer rules the Lackawanna Valley, but for visitors who come seeking the story of the miners and their lives, the rich heritage of the past has been preserved.

Scranton is an ideal place to begin your journey back in time. With five major rail lines with direct connections to principal cities of the East Coast and Canada, Scranton in the 1800s grew to a major industrial center, where mining, iron and steel, rails, textiles, and manufacturing combined to produce a thriving economy.

Leaving I-81, you follow Keyser Avenue south to McDade Park on the shoulder of Bald Mountain. At the Lackawanna Coal Mine Tour office, buy your ticket and prepare for an extraordinary experience as you descend into the abandoned #190 slope of the Continental Mine. The cable cars you ride are the same as those that served the miners, and your guide is likely to be a former miner or a member of his family. Reaching the base of the shaft, you follow the group, shivering in the fifty-two-degree dampness, and learn about the dangerous and physically demanding work of the mines. Returning to the surface, you wonder at the fortitude of the men who tolerated these working conditions every day of their lives, and you make a silent vow never to complain about your job again.

Just uphill from the mine, the state Anthracite Heritage Museum explores the history, culture, ethnic diversity, and religious impact that immigrants had on the region. Starting with paleo-Indians, the exhibits trace the pattern of immigration from past to present through old photographs and simple artifacts, such as a breaker boy's hobnail boots.

Not only coal mining but textile manufacturing is featured. If you've ever wondered how Victorian lace curtains are made, check out the Nottingham Lace Loom from the Scranton Lace Company.

Across town on the banks of Roaring Brook, the four massive stone stacks of the Lackawanna Iron and Coal Company's blast furnaces still stand at the Scranton Iron Furnaces site. One of the first American ironworks to manufacture the T rail so essential to railroading, the company's furnaces and the iron that flowed from them were instrumental to the growth of the city. Today the parklike locale is administered by the state Historical and Museum Commission, and interpretive signing aids the visitor in understanding the process that transformed ore, limestone, and coal into iron and, after the addition of Bessemer converters, into steel.

A few blocks from the furnaces, the National Park Service has turned the derelict Delaware Lackawanna & Western (DL&W) rail yards into Steamtown, a National Historic Site established "to further public understanding and appreciation of the development of steam locomotives in the region." A park in the making, it is scheduled to open in the first quarter of 1995.

Watching the new buildings take shape is exciting. The renovated Roundhouse is joined by the North and South Exhibit Buildings and the Visitors Center and Theater, all of which form a ring of construction circling the working turntable. The old Oil House will be cleaned up, shored up, and transformed into a permanent bookshop. The park's entrance will be changed from its temporary location on Washington Avenue to a site adjacent to the Visitors Center.

In the meantime there is plenty to excite both the hardcore rail fan and the casual visitor. From Memorial Day to the end of October, a yard shuttle operates daily, and tours to the iron furnaces run on weekends. From July Fourth weekend to

15

the end of foliage season, special excursions steam the twenty-five-mile round-trip between Scranton and Moscow.

At the active Roundhouse and turntable (the largest working one of its kind in the country), you may watch steam locomotives being readied for "the road." Visitors to the shops will see restorers actively working on the park's rolling stock, which includes treasures such as one of two existing DL&W 2-6-0 Moguls from the Schenectady works of the American Locomotive Company or the massive Union Pacific 4-8-8-4 "Big Boy," more than 132 feet long and weighing 1.2 million pounds.

If you've been touring Steamtown and want a quick sandwich, stop at nearby Smith's Restaurant on Cedar Avenue (US 11). The unpretentious eatery has been owned by the same family for more than fifty years, and their menu lists a variety of light eating from chunk tuna served with fresh fruit to sliced top round or fresh ham on a hard roll. Daily specials run from a roast chicken dinner to spareribs and sauerkraut, and for dessert their tapioca pudding is a sure winner.

As proof that the citizens of the coal region value art as well as industry, the Everhart Museum in Nay Aug Park has a splendid collection of nineteenth- and twentieth-century paintings, with additional displays of Dorflinger glass, American folk art, and Oriental and ethnographic art. The natural history exhibits include Dinosaur Hall, a large collection of rare and extinct birds, and a living beehive.

Scranton's landmark hostelry is the Lackawanna Station Hotel. Built in 1908 to house the DL&W railroad station, the French Renaissance structure is a sterling example of adaptive reuse of a building too good for the wrecking ball. Elegant guest rooms are complemented by the gracious public areas. The main lobby is richly ornamented with brown, pink, and green Italian marble; and the thirty-six faience panels ringing the ceiling depict the landscapes of a railroad journey from

Buffalo, New York, to Hoboken, New Jersey. Carmen's full-service restaurant takes complete advantage of its location off the beautiful main lobby; the Lackawanna Station Restaurant and Bar provide more casual dining.

For a meal at a Scranton "classic," go to Cooper's Seafood House on North Washington Avenue. Don't be deceived by the outside—a boat swarming with pirates and topped by a sinister giant octopus. This is no tourist trap but a popular restaurant as comfortable for visiting celebrities as for family groups. The selection of briny denizens ranges from Maryland crab cakes to Mississippi catfish fillets, with appetizer oddities such as shark bites and alligator tenderloin. The interior decor varies from a one-ton, twenty-five-foot replica of a blue whale in the Whale Room to an HO train that chugs around a ceiling track in the Captain's Room.

Leaving Scranton, you can follow US 11 south through the communities of Moosic, Duryea, and Avoca, or avoid stop-and-go traffic by dodging out to I-81 for twenty-eight miles. The journey between the Dorrance exit and North Hazleton is through open country, but as you approach Hazleton, keep your eyes peeled for State 940, where you turn left at the Shell station. On your journey to Eckley you'll see some of the less lovely aspects of coal mining: mountains of mine residue, or culm, dotting the landscape; skeletons of old coal breakers; and black-silt ponds. Like a crazy quilt, these scars on the terrain are mixed with sections of mountain beauty: forested hills and wildflowers blooming by the roadside.

Eckley Miners' Village is a bona fide coal patch community, an example of the company-owned towns that provided homes to miners during the Anthracite era. Part of the state's Anthracite Museum Complex, the village is a living museum still tenanted by miners, their wives or widows, and their children.

*The anthracite breaker in Eckley, a reminder of
coal-mining days*

A breaker, constructed for Paramount Studio's filming of
The Molly Maguires, dominates the skyline. In structures such
as this, young boys once picked slate from coal for long hours
and short pay. Visitors may stroll the central street and visit
the Roman Catholic Church of the Immaculate Conception,
St. James' Protestant Episcopal Church, a miner's furnished
double dwelling, the doctor's office, and the Company Store,
which houses the gift shop.

The visitors center introduces life in the village with a
slide show and exhibits on the town's history and on the
home life of the miner and his wife and children. Here you
may sign on with a knowledgeable guide or pick up material
for a solitary stroll.

The village of Jim Thorpe is a good overnight stop on
your way to Ashland. Once three feuding boroughs—Mauch
Chunk, Upper Mauch Chunk, and East Mauch Chunk—the
town was formed into one city in 1954, when the widow of the

great Native American athlete offered her husband's name and body as a uniting symbol, in exchange for a proper memorial.

Thorpe's twenty-ton pink granite mausoleum overlooks the old Victorian coal town with its Millionaires Row, hillside mansions, and distinctive 1893 Carbon County Courthouse. Shops of all varieties line Broadway, and you can buy everything from a country-crafted basket to an antique toothpick holder. Overlooking the town, the Asa Packer Mansion is a twenty-room Italianate villa that was the home of the pioneer and founder of the Lehigh Valley Railroad and Lehigh University. Preserved with all its elaborately carved wood paneling and original furnishings, it is open to the public for tours.

Up on Race Street, Saint Mark's Episcopal Church has spectacular Tiffany windows and an original English Minton tile floor. Beyond the church, a tiny lane hosts colorful small shops housed in three-story stone row houses originally built for the engineers and foremen of the Lehigh Valley Railroad.

For a quick meal, try the Sunrise Diner, where you can sup inside or join the group on the deck. The food's not fancy, but it's honest and filling. If you need a bed and breakfast, consider The Inn at Jim Thorpe, an 1840 hotel and restaurant restored to its original Victorian elegance. The rooms are exceptionally well-appointed with fine furnishings and all the comforts of home, including air conditioning, TV, and room phones.

From Jim Thorpe to Ashland is a distance of thirty-six miles through typical coal country, a land of blemished beauty. On a hill above town, the state's third anthracite museum features a diverse collection of tools, machinery, and photographs depicting the actual process of coal mining. Exhibits and equipment span the time from the era of pick and shovel to today's mining techniques.

The museum is joined by the Pioneer Tunnel Coal Mine and Lokie Ride, a community-sponsored attraction that allows visitors to see an actual horizontal drift mine, which runs straight into the heart of Mahanoy Mountain. Guides are frequently miners, who patiently explain how mining in this part of the coal fields differed from what you observed in Scranton.

The steam lokie is actually an old mine engine, which once took ore from strip mines to the breaker. On its three-quarter-mile run, you will see the Mammoth Stripping, an area where the Mammoth Vein bent to the surface, and immense steam shovels ripped millions of tons of coal from solid rock.

Your last look at coal country as you head north to Bloomsburg is Centralia, that notorious town where the ground burns. The fire, started accidentally when a surface coal seam ignited, smolders on in spite of massive efforts at eradication. Centralia must have been a pretty town, sitting high on the ridge, but there's not a whole lot left of the village. Many row houses have been torn down, leaving odd brick abutments to support those still inhabited by residents unwilling to abandon their homes.

Leaving these gutsy survivors, you're impressed not so much by the afflictions of coal country but rather with the remarkable resilience of its people. The hope of the region rests where it always has, in the energy of the men and women who mined anthracite, built rail lines, and powered industry. Their legacy of resourcefulness is the key to the future.

In the Area

All numbers are within area code 717 unless otherwise indicated.

Lackawanna Coal Mine Tour, Scranton, 963-MINE. May through November. Fee.

Anthracite Heritage Museum, Scranton, 963-4804. Fee.

Scranton Iron Furnaces, Scranton, 963-3208.

Steamtown National Historic Site, Scranton, 961-2033.
Guided tours year-round; other tours seasonal. Fee for
excursions.

Smith's Restaurant, Scranton, 961-9192. Closed Sunday.

Everhart Museum, Scranton, 346-8370. Closed Monday.
Donation.

Lackawanna Station Hotel, Scranton, 800-347-6888 or
342-8300.

Cooper's Seafood House, Scranton, 346-6883.

Eckley Miners' Village, Eckley, 636-2070 or 636-2071. Fee.

Asa Packer Mansion, Jim Thorpe, 325-3229. May 15 through
October 31. Fee.

Saint Mark's Episcopal Church, Jim Thorpe, 325-4883. Daily
from May 15 through October 31. Fee.

Sunrise Diner, Jim Thorpe, 325-4093.

The Inn at Jim Thorpe, Jim Thorpe, 325-2599.

Museum of Anthracite Mining, Ashland, 875-4708. Daily
from May 1 through October 31. Closed Monday from
November 1 through April 30. Fee.

Pioneer Tunnel Coal Mine and Steam Train, Ashland,
875-3850 or 875-3301. Daily from Memorial Day through
Labor Day weekend. Weekends in May and from Labor
Day through October. Fee.

Pennsylvania's Northeast Territory Visitors Bureau, Avoca
(Scranton), 800-735-2629 or 457-1320.

Carbon County Tourist Promotion Agency, Jim Thorpe,
325-3673.

Schuylkill County Visitors Bureau, Pottsville (Ashland),
800-765-7282 or 622-7700.

3 ~

River Road Journey

Getting there: Take the Pennsylvania Turnpike to US 13.

Highlights: *A sojourn of two or more days in Bucks County takes you from William Penn's home on the Delaware River to the Historic Fallsington, the "town time forgot," and on to the site of Gen. George Washington's crossing of the Delaware. Visit the old colonial towns of Newtown and Doylestown, the latter with a museum, castle, and tile works commemorating the genius of an eccentric and innovative millionaire.*

The Route

From I-276 (I-76), the Pennsylvania Turnpike, take the Delaware Valley exit 29 near the Pennsylvania/New Jersey border to US 13 north. Turn right, or southeast, on Green Lane Road and north, or left, on Radcliff Street, which becomes Old Main Street and Bordentown Road. Cross Scotts Creek and turn south on Pennsbury Road. From Pennsbury Manor, exit Pennsbury Road, turn right on Bordentown Road and left on New Ford Road. Go left on Tyburn to US 1 east and Fallsington. From Fallsington follow US 1 east to State 32, the River

Road, north to Washington Crossing. Take State 532 west to Newtown, State 413 north, State 263 south, and State 313 north to Doylestown. Alternatively, take State 611 from exit 27 of the Pennsylvania Turnpike at Willow Grove north to Doylestown. The total River Road tour is about forty-seven miles.

North of Philadelphia the industrial Delaware River undergoes a startling transformation. Gone are the docks, the soaring bridges, the busy waterfronts. In their stead are wetlands crowned with grassy reeds and marshes intersected by twisting streams. Ducks nest in protected backwaters, and muskrat make their burrows along the muddy banks.

Twenty-six miles upstream from Center City, Pennsylvania's founder built his country estate. For his own home William Penn chose a site far from the heat and bustle of Philadelphia. At a time when roads were primitive and transport by boat was easier, the site in lower Bucks County well suited his needs.

In 1682 he began construction, which was supervised by his steward when politics called Penn back to England. He was not destined to long enjoy the magnificent two-story brick Georgian manor house, the verdant lawns sweeping down to the river, the commodious barns, formal gardens, orchards, and vineyards. Penn's time in the New World was short: from 1682 to 1684 and again from 1699 to 1701.

Through the decades the estate fell into disrepair. By 1929 no trace of Pennsbury survived, and nineteenth-century buildings covered the original foundations. In 1932 the Charles Warner Company gave ten acres, including the area of the original structures, to the Commonwealth, and from 1933 to 1942 the state Historical Commission reconstructed the plantation, including the house, outbuildings, and landscape. Even the gardens were taken from Penn's original instructions and careful archaeological excavations.

Visiting Pennsbury today is a felicitous journey, especially during spring and summer when Horned Dorset lambs gambol on the lawns, Red Devon cattle low in the paddock, and the gardens are in their glory. Roses, hyacinth bean, and love-lies-bleeding bloom in the Upper Court, where Penn walked with his guests; the kitchen and herb gardens produce an abundance of savories and comestibles.

Although strolling the grounds any day brings rewards, "Sundays at Pennsbury" are especially enticing. From 1:00 P.M. to 4:00 P.M. between April and October, Pennsbury stages living history programs ranging from cooking and baking over an open hearth to woodworking and blacksmithing at the joyner [sic] and smithy's shops.

The visitors center is the place for a general orientation to the property and a chance to arrange for a period-costumed guide, whose massive iron key unlocks the doors of the manor house and whose well-honed documentary unlocks many of the secrets of Pennsbury's historic forty-three acres.

Leaving Pennsbury, you are thrust rather rudely back into the modern world. The surrounding wetlands are home to wildlife, but they are also the site of several industrial complexes and landfills. Heavy trucks lumber along these two-lane roads, making driving an exercise in caution. After surviving the back roads and US 1, the turnoff to Historic Fallsington comes as a welcome respite.

One of the earliest settlements in Pennsylvania, Fallsington has survived the passing of time and the encroachment of modern suburban expansion. It is a miracle of preservation in a sea of shopping malls and superhighways and a monument to the wisdom and perspicacity of residents who didn't allow progress to bulldoze their heritage.

The first homes in Fallsington were built by friends and followers of William Penn, and it was not unusual for Penn to ride from Pennsbury to Falls Meeting for Sunday services. The village's inherent charm is apparent to even the casual visitor, but it is of special interest in its role as a mirror of 300

24

years of American architectural history, from a log cabin of the seventeenth century to the frills and furbelows of the Victorian nineteenth century.

The heart of Fallsington is Meetinghouse Square, where the stone and frame houses, tavern, store, and other buildings cluster. This is not a static re-creation; most of the homes are occupied with current proud residents. Four buildings are open to the public, with a formal guided tour initiating at Gillingham Store with an audiovisual presentation and progressing to the 1685 Moon-Williamson log house, the 1790 Stage Coach Tavern, and the 1758 Schoolmaster's House.

From the tranquility of Fallsington, it is only a short ride on busy US 1 before the intersection with River Road in Morrisville. Heading north, you leave densely settled lower Bucks County, and by the time you reach Yardley, the route is pleasantly pastoral with the Delaware slipping along to your right. The Yardley Inn, once a colonial tavern, is a pleasant place for lunch, with its porch dining room overlooking the stream.

Four miles north is McConkey's Ferry, the spot that Gen. George Washington chose to launch a sneak attack against the Hessians at Trenton on Christmas night 1776. It was a desperate gamble. After the defeat at the Battle of Long Island and other setbacks, the Continental army had retreated across New Jersey with the British in pursuit. With morale at its lowest ebb since the start of the campaign, Washington needed a victory; his daring plan was to cross the ice-choked river under cover of darkness and attack occupied Trenton from the north. Washington's plan worked, and every Christmas Day the stirring drama is reenacted by costumed men in Durham boats at Washington Crossing Historic Park.

The park, which is administered by the state Historical and Museum Commission in cooperation with The Washington Crossing Park Commission, has two geographic sections and three distinct characters. McConkey's Ferry Section begins where State 532 crosses into New Jersey. Here you'll find the keystone-shaped Memorial Building and Visitors Center, which houses a revolutionary period museum and an auditorium where you'll see a heroically sized replica of Emanuel Leutze's famous painting, "Washington Crossing the Delaware."

Between the bridge and the Visitors Center lies the old town of Taylorsville. Costumed guides from the Visitors Center shepherd visitors around the collection of modest early homes; the Durham boat house; Homewood, a restored nineteenth-century residence; and the Taylorsville store, a popular spot for thirsty bikers and avid souvenir hunters. The Inn at McConkey's Ferry is a must-see, because it was in this tavern that General Washington and his aides supped before embarking on their historic journey.

The Thompson's Mill section lies just three and a half miles north of the McConkey's Ferry Section. This eighteenth-century farm and industrial complex includes a colonial barn, a gristmill, and the Thompson-Neely house, home of the Pidcock, Thompson, and Neely families from 1702 to 1858, and the headquarters of Maj. Gen. Lord Stirling, who in 1776 was stationed on the Delaware to prevent British troops crossing.

A dedicated wildflower preserve of 100 acres is directly across the road; the woodlands and meadows are especially spectacular in spring when trillium and lady's slipper bloom. Miles of paths include a self-guided nature trail, a fern and club moss trail, a sphagnum bog, and a trail featuring medicinal plants.

A short detour up Lurgan Road takes you to the access road to Bowman's Tower, a 100-foot observation column built in 1930 to commemorate a Revolutionary War lookout point. A modern elevator whisks you to the top, where you can see New Hope to the north and, on a clear day, the Pennsylvania/ New Jersey turnpike bridge to the south.

B. DALTON BOOKSELLER
518 CAMP HILLSHOP CTR, CAMPHILL, PA

REG#01   CLERK 023   RECEIPT#   30458
06/13/94   11:13 AM

S 1566260329   COUNTRY ROADS OF PA
1 @ 9.95   9.95

S 0517880903   AWAY FOR THE WEEKEND MID
1 @ 15.00 15.00

SUBTOTAL	24.95
CARD SAVINGS - 10%	-2.50
CARD # 119278119812991299	
DISCOUNTED SUBTOTAL	22.45
SALES TAX - 6%	1.35
TOTAL	23.80
CASH PAYMENT	50.00
CHANGE	26.20

LIST   24.95 SELL   22.45

YOU SAVED   2.50
THANK YOU FOR SHOPPING AT B. DALTON!

Leaving the park, you have the option of heading north into New Hope, a bustling town of shops, galleries, and, during the season, lots and lots of tourists, or backtracking to State 532 for a drive west to Newtown, a 300-year-old village with the largest historic district in a very historic county.

Newtown dates back to the time of William Penn, with 230 structures on the National Historic Register, including four eighteenth-century taverns. There are comfortable hostelries, good restaurants, and a sprinkling of antique shops. Best of all, there is a lack of pretense. The historical society prints a walking tour, but that's about as involved as it gets. The village is a low-key place to unwind; one of the best places to relax and renew is the veranda dining room of The Brick Hotel.

The Brick was twelve years old when General Washington and his troops took sustenance there. In 1828 Joseph Archambault, aid to Napoleon Bonaparte, expanded the hotel to its present size, and in the ensuing years The Brick flourished as a haven for Victorian drummers and entrepreneurs. One of Newtown's signature structures, the hotel has been thoroughly modernized. Its public rooms are high Victorian and its bedrooms and suites are elegant and comfortable.

Newtown to Doylestown is a short hop through rural landscape dotted with sod plantations and the estates of gentlemen farmers. On the outskirts of the city stand three medieval-looking reinforced concrete "castles." Situated within little more than a mile of each other, they were built by a renaissance man, Dr. Henry Chapman Mercer, whose concepts and techniques of building were a century ahead of his time. On a superficial level, Mercer was an eccentric. He studied to become a lawyer but instead spent his life in the study of archaeology, anthropology, ceramics, and historical research. His greatest work was his comprehensive collection, *Tools of the Nationmaker*, which chronicled American history through common working implements.

To house his encyclopedic collection, Mercer constructed his museum in 1916. Words fail when attempting to describe the building and its contents. Museum staff members have been known to refer to the Great Hall as the "Oh, my God!" room, after the usual reaction. Tools used for more than fifty crafts and occupations are displayed in four tiers of alcoves that open on a main court, the ceiling and sides of which are hung with baskets, stagecoaches, boats, a Conestoga wagon, and the like.

Mercer's home, Fonthill, utilizes the same reinforced concrete construction and showcases his talent as a tilemaker and a leader in America's arts and crafts movement. Working without blueprints, Mercer improvised the entire structure, embellishing the floors and ceilings of the twenty-seven-room mansion with his endless collection of prints and mosaic epics from his pottery. The effect is both bizarre and theatrical.

The third building of the "Mercer Mile" is the Moravian Pottery & Tile Works, which, during its years of operation, produced decorative tiles for such important installations as the Pennsylvania state capitol, Boston's Gardner Museum, and the John D. Rockefeller estate in New York. Purchased by Bucks County and established as a museum, it is a functioning pottery works open for tours. A well-stocked gift shop carries modern reproductions of the Mercer patterns.

Not part of the Mercer story but a worthy extension to the Doylestown circuit, the James A. Michener Art Museum occupies a site across the street from The Mercer Museum. It is named for one of the city's most illustrious sons. The art museum is housed in the former county jail, with its arched entrance dividing the original warden's house, a three-story Gothic structure. The center sculpture court is brightened with beds of flowers, with the galleries and exhibition spaces radiating out in a semicircle backed by the old thirty-foot-high prison wall. A recent expansion has added gallery space, a museum shop, a tearoom, and a children's gallery. The

Fonthill, a twenty-seven-room mansion built by
Henry Chapman Mercer

museum's main focus is its permanent collection of works by
nineteenth- and twentieth-century Pennsylvania Impression-
ists, although touring exhibitions of both national and regional interest are provided display space.

After a full day on tour, it's time to head downtown for dinner before seeking out a comfy bed and breakfast. For the pasta aficionado, Paganini Ristorante at 72 West State Street specializes in fresh, homemade pastas and sauces and daily specials, such as Saturday's *tagliatelle di fruitti di marre*, with fresh mussels, shrimp, herbs, and tomato. Sit back, enjoy a glass of *vino*, and dip the hearty warm-crusted bread in the saucer of extravirgin olive oil provided at every table.

With the inner being well-satisfied, head out Lower State Road to Pine Tree Farm, where Roy and Joy Feigles have a 16.5-acre bit of heaven complete with swimming pool, tennis courts, and a pond with resident greeting bullfrog. The original stucco farmhouse was built in 1730, and the stone addition has only added to the building's charm. One of Joy's forebears came over on the *Welcome* with William Penn, and this gracious lady really knows how to welcome guests.

Another excellent Doylestown bed and breakfast is Highland Farms, the former estate of lyricist Oscar Hammerstein II. Each guest bedroom in the stone and stucco eighteenth-century home is named for a musical and is furnished with antiques and Hammerstein memorabilia. There's a sixty-foot pool shaped like Hammerstein's favorite fruit (a pear), and a wide wraparound porch for lazing away the remainder of a sunny afternoon. Host Mary Schnitzer's warm personality pervades the house, and her tasty country breakfasts leave guests well prepared for another day exploring country roads.

In the Area

All numbers are within area code 215.

Pennsbury Manor, Morrisville, 946-0400. Closed Mondays and holidays except Memorial Day, July 4, and Labor Day. Fee. Tours last an hour and a half.

Historic Fallsington, Fallsington, 295-6567. Daily from May
through November. Fee. Call for tour appointment.

The Yardley Inn, Yardley, 493-3800.

Washington Crossing Historic Park, Washington Crossing.
493-4076. Fee.

The Brick Hotel, Newtown, 860-8313. Restaurant open daily
for lunch and dinner; Saturday breakfast and Sunday
brunch. Lodging open daily.

Newtown Historical Association, Inc., P.O. Box 303,
Newtown, PA 18940.

The Mercer Museum, Doylestown, 345-0210. Daily from
March through December. Fee.

Fonthill Museum, Doylestown, 348-9461. Daily from March
through December. Call for tour hours. Fee.

Moravian Pottery & Tile Works, Doylestown, 345-6722.
Tours Wednesday through Sunday from March through
December. Fee.

James A. Michener Art Museum, Doylestown, 340-9800.
Closed Monday. Fee.

Paganini Ristorante, Doylestown, 348-5922.

Pine Tree Farm, Doylestown, 348-0632.

Highland Farms, Doylestown, 340-1354.

Bucks County Tourist Commission, Doylestown, 345-4552 or
800-836-2825.

4 ~

South Central Homelands

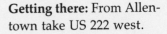

Getting there: From Allentown take US 222 west.

Highlights: *Take a weekend to explore Rodale Institute Research Center's organic gardens, Renninger's Antiques and Farmers' Market in Kutztown, Crystal Cave's underground passages, and Hawk Mountain's display of migrating birds of prey. Ride the Blue Mountain & Reading Railroad and tour the beautiful Oley Valley. Visit Daniel Boone's birthplace and a nineteenth-century "iron plantation."*

The Route

From Allentown, take US 222 west to Maxatawny and turn right for Rodale on Sigfreidville Road. Regain US 222 west, then take State 737 south to Kutztown. Go south on Noble Street for Renninger's. Return to US 222 west and follow it to the Virginville exit. Take State 143 north to SR 1006 west, Crystal Cave Road. Leaving the cave, continue west on Crystal Cave Road to its intersection with State 143 north at Virginville. Take State 143 and pass under I-78. At the intersection of Hawk Mountain Road and Stony Creek, turn west for the sanctuary or east for the B & B.

Follow Hawk Mountain Road west until it dead-ends, and turn south on State 895 and south again on State 61 through Port Clinton, crossing I-78 to Hamburg and Shoemakersville. Take State 662 east to State 143/662 southeast through Oley to Yellow House and turn west on State 562 to SR 2041 south, Daniel Boone Road. Leaving the park, proceed south to US 422 (to turn east on US 422, you must first go west, then south on State 82). After accessing US 422 east, take State 724 east and State 345 south to Hopewell. Continue south on State 345 to State 23 west and State 10 north to Morgantown and Pennsylvania Turnpike exit 22. The approximate total miles is eighty-nine.

When fall's scarlet and gold dapple the hills and the corn stands in shocks in the field, take a weekend to explore one of the state's most unspoiled and least appreciated areas. Pennsylvania's rural south central homelands stretch between Allentown and Harrisburg, where traffic thins and sporadic exits mark towns with names such as Kutztown or Krumsville. Off-highway hex signs decorate Teutonic bank barns, and the people with strong German or "Dutch" accents still shepherd the land descended to them from early Pennsylvania Dutch settlers, who were neither Amish nor Mennonite but just simple farmers.

Your first stop is the Rodale Institute Research Center, one of the world's leading research facilities for organic horticulture and sustainable agriculture. In operation since 1972, the 333-acre farm is a model for innovative farming and gardening systems without the aid of chemical fertilizers or pesticides.

Home to the Johannes Siegfried family for nine generations from the time of William Penn until 1966, the land has been lovingly tended. Whether or not you're a serious gardener, you'll enjoy strolling the grounds on a self-guided tour or going into more detail with a knowledgeable guide. If you can tear yourself away from the Siegfriedale Schoolhouse, which holds the visitors center and a well-stocked bookstore cum gift shop, you'll have the opportunity to learn the latest in organic gardening techniques and visit the demonstration garden, where new vegetable and flower varieties are tested each year. There's even a children's garden.

If you're passing near Kutztown on Friday or Saturday, be sure to stop at Renninger's Antiques and Farmers' Market. Although the mart is one of the finest in the area and stocks a varied array of products, from Pennsylvania Dutch treats to basic staples, Renninger's is best known for its Antique & Flea Market. Every Saturday more than 250 booths lure shoppers with a wide selection of china, furniture, dolls, sports memorabilia, and the like. Action begins outdoors at dawn for some eager shoppers who dart from table to table with flashlights.

Renninger's pulls out all the stops for its famous Antique Extravaganzas in April, June, and September. Drawing nearly 1,200 dealers from forty-two states, the sales are a frenzy of buying and selling. Crowds throng to Kutztown and booths spill out of the permanent buildings to cover acres of adjoining fields.

If you're not claustrophobic and you don't mind a bit of stair and ramp climbing, visit nearby Crystal Cave. Discovered in 1871 by two Pennsylvania Dutchmen working on a stone quarry, the limestone cavern has been a local attraction since David Kohler made the entrance accessible and opened a hotel for visitors shortly thereafter. There is the inevitable gift shop, food stands, miniature golf, and rock shop, but the star is the cave itself, which nature has graced with an abundance of stalactites, stalagmites, and dripstone in shades ranging from white to iron-tinted cream.

Heading north beyond I-78, Hawk Mountain Road intersects with State 143. If the day is winding down and you're searching for comfortable quarters, turn right on Stony Run for Hawk Mountain Inn. Built by owners Jim and Judy Gaffney in 1988, the fieldstone inn has eight units with all the modern amenities and a comfortable Commons Room, where guests gather for breakfast and evening activities. The first floor of the Gaffney home houses a fine restaurant serving five-course dinners Thursday through Saturday plus Sunday brunch. A screened porch looking over the pond and swimming pool is a warm weather alternative to the two cozy dining rooms.

On evenings that the inn doesn't serve dinner, Jim will suggest alternatives. The Kempton Hotel is a colorful option. An 1874 country tavern with a basic menu featuring Pennsylvania Dutch specials, the Kempton is best known for its handpainted ceilings. The dining room highlights American historic scenes; the bar features local scenes, including one of Willie Nelson's early appearances in the small village.

In the morning after a hearty breakfast, head out to Hawk Mountain Sanctuary, stopping on the way to visit Willi Singleton at Pine Creek Pottery. This talented artisan specializes in distinctive pottery made from local materials, wood-flame fired in a unique four-chambered Mashiko-style Japanese climbing kiln. Willi is enthusiastic about his work and enjoys showing visitors about.

If it's a brisk fall day with a northwest wind, Hawk Mountain is at its most spectacular, with hundreds of birds of prey soaring over Kittatiny Ridge, on the raptors' southern migration route. A private, member-supported, 2,200-acre wildlife refuge, Hawk Mountain is one of Pennsylvania's true treasures.

In the early part of this century, as today, people were drawn to witness the spectacular migration, but then the crowds consisted mostly of gunners intent on slaughtering as many hawks as possible. In 1932 photographer and naturalist Richard Pough pictorially recorded the carnage. These photographs motivated conservationist Rosalie Edge to buy approximately 1,400 acres where the shooting occurred and establish the sanctuary.

Today thousands of hawks, falcons, and eagles fly by the lookouts unmolested on their journey to wintering grounds as distant as Central and South America. Utilizing energy-saving strategies for taking advantage of localized air currents, they ride thermals, or updrafts, created when winds coming from the northwest hit the ridge.

Visitors to the sanctuary should stop at the visitors center, where they'll find exhibits of the many raptor species, an explanation of the dynamics of migration, and a gift shop with a selection of reference books, field guides, and avian keepsakes. Across the road, the trail to North Lookout, the most popular spotting location, is three-fourths of mile, with numerous overlooks and side trails along the way. Parts of the path are very rocky, so sturdy footwear is strongly advised. In addition, the rocky promontory is buffeted by winds and can be considerably colder than the woods. A warm jacket is in order plus a sit-upon to cushion rocks. Many enthusiasts bring binoculars, lunches, and a thermos of something hot to drink.

In addition to the lookouts, there are several hiking trails, including access to the Appalachian Trail and the rugged "River of Rocks," a 3.5-mile trek down a boulder field. A habitat area provides another type of bird-watching environment, with two ponds, waterfalls, a marsh, and native wildflowers and shrubs.

Leaving the sanctuary, you eventually emerge on busy State 61 and travel through the little town of Port Clinton, where you'll find some of the best freshly roasted goobers anywhere at The Peanut Shop.

Directly after crossing I-78, you take a journey back into the golden age of railroading on the Blue Mountain & Reading

Rural Pennsylvania mailboxes

Railroad at South Hamburg. It's time to hop aboard when that lonesome whistle blows, and the 404-ton engine No. 2102 pulls out of the station for the journey to Temple. The standard gauge short line, originally a segment of the Schuylkill

Division of the Pennsylvania Railroad, runs through twenty-six miles of farmland with views of the old Schuylkill Canal and Maiden Creek. The narrated trip takes an hour and a half: half an hour to Temple, a half-hour stop at the Temple station, and half an hour for the return. Special events are scheduled from Easter to Christmas, including the popular fall foliage runs all the way to Jim Thorpe in the Poconos.

From Hamburg, your driving route takes a series of twists and turns through the beautiful, unspoiled Oley Valley. In Oley proper, the 1881 Oley Valley Inn, with its American cuisine with a Continental flair and its graceful decor, draws diners from as far distant as Philadelphia. Owner/chef Steve Yeanish takes pride in using fresh ingredients and herbs from the garden to create specialties such as sesame baked Atlantic salmon fillet and Black Forest–style veal tenderloin with Westphalian ham, morels, apple schnapps, and cream.

Near the southern extremity of Berks County and just a few miles east of Reading, the birthplace of frontiersman Daniel Boone stands on 579 acres of woods, meadows, and waterways. The Daniel Boone Homestead, a state historical park, has changed since Quaker Squire Boone purchased the original 200 acres in 1730. Other families acquired the land and made improvements, and the Boone cabin evolved through the years into a two-story stone and frame farmhouse. Various outbuildings were constructed, including a smokehouse, blacksmith shop, bank barn, the Bertolet log house and bake house, sawmill, and cemetery. The park, which serves as a wildlife refuge in addition to its interpretive function, is a peaceful, bucolic spot, with picnic groves and paths for strolling. The visitors center houses a series of exhibits, a museum shop, and a tour desk.

Leaving the Homestead, you do a confusing series of turns to cross US 422 and head south, but once beyond Birdsboro, it's clear sailing. Several miles out of town on the Birdsboro-Hopewell Road, you pass into French Creek State Park, 7,339 acres of woods and meadows with two lakes for boating and fishing; an immense swimming pool for summer bathing; 32 miles of hiking trails, including 6.5 miles of the popular Horseshoe Trail; and a generous supply of picnic areas in spots both shaded and sunny.

Surrounded on three sides by the park, Hopewell Furnace National Historic Site has been restored to its original condition as an early American iron-making community. The visitors center houses exhibits, push-button videos, and a ten-minute slide show. The building is flanked by a 300-tree apple orchard (where picking is encouraged), which in the fall offers a bounteous harvest of traditional and historic varieties. For a token fee, you can take home as many bushels of Starrs, Staymans, or any of the other twenty-one varieties as you can carry. Orchard windfalls attract hungry deer, and a large herd frequently browses under the trees.

Following the self-guided paths through the community, you are struck by how clean and green everything appears. Such was not the case when the furnace was "in blast." In summer, living history demonstrations recreate the late nineteenth century, and although the night-and-day roar of the forced air blast furnace is gone forever, the sound of the blacksmith's anvil and the clack of the loom help visitors imagine the era.

Hopewell is actually older than the time portrayed. Its first ironmaster, Mark Bird, chose the location because of its proximity to both roads and the necessary raw materials—iron ore, limestone, and hardwood for charcoal. From 1771 to 1883, the furnace produced pig iron and finished castings, and during the Revolutionary War it manufactured cannon, shot, and shell for the Continental army. Hopewell's most prosperous period was from 1820 to 1840, when the workers turned out pots, kettles, machinery, grates, and the plates for wood-burning stoves.

There is much to see: the massive furnace and the ponderous waterwheel, which provided compressed air through a system of pistons and wooden "blowing tubs," the elegant ironmaster's house, company store, schoolhouse, blacksmith's shop, model charcoal hearth and cooling sheds, church, barn, smokehouse, and tenant houses with kitchen gardens. For the history maven or the casual tourist, several hours at Hopewell is well spent. As you head back to I-78, you will remember your sojourn into a fascinating but little explored section of the Commonwealth.

In the Area

All numbers are within area code 215 unless otherwise indicated.

Rodale Institute Research Center, Maxatawny, 683-6383.
    Daily; one-hour tours from May 1 to October 31. Fee.

Renninger's Antiques and Farmers' Market, Kutztown, 717-385-0104. Monday through Thursday, 683-6848. Farmers' Market on Friday and Saturday; Antique Market on Saturday.

Crystal Cave, Kutztown, 683-6765. March through November. Fee.

Pine Creek Pottery, Kempton, 756-6387.

The Hawk Mountain Inn, Kempton, 756-4224.
    Accommodations daily. Restaurant Friday and Saturday for dinner, Sunday for brunch.

The Kempton Hotel, Kempton, 756-6588. Closed Tuesday.

Hawk Mountain Sanctuary, Kempton, 756-6961. Fee.

The Peanut Shop, Port Clinton, 562-0610. Wednesday through Sunday from January through October, plus Monday and Tuesday in November and December.

The Blue Mountain & Reading Railroad, South Hamburg. Office, Monday through Friday, 562-4083; station, weekends, 562-5224. Daily from July 1 through Labor Day; open Friday through Sunday from early May through June 30 and Labor Day through the end of October. Fee.

The Oley Valley Inn, Oley, 987-6400. Dinner Tuesday through Saturday, Sunday brunch.

Daniel Boone Homestead, Birdsboro, 582-4900. Closed Monday. Fee.

French Creek State Park, Elverson 582-1514.

Hopewell Furnace National Historic Site, Elverson, 582-8773 or 582-2093. Allow an hour and a half for tour. Fee.

Reading & Berks County Visitors Bureau, Wyomissing, 800-443-6610 or 375-4085.

5 ~

The Other Lancaster

Getting there: From York and Lancaster take US 30 to State 72 south.

Highlights: *Lancaster is both a bustling, modern city and a largely agrarian county. On this two-day journey, you'll explore some sights missed by the casual visitor to the tourist meccas in and around heavily traveled US 30. Your itinerary begins at Lancaster's fabled Central Market and continues on to President James Buchanan's home, Wheatlands. You visit a living museum of country life in rural Landis Valley, the early German monastic settlement of Ephrata Cloisters, and the multifaceted Moravian village of Lititz. Step lively and bring your appetite!*

The Route

From US 30 linking the cities of York and Lancaster, take State 72 south (in Lancaster State 72 becomes Prince Street). Turn east on King Street (State 462) to Penn Square. From Penn Square, follow Queen Street north to Orange Street west to State 23 west to Rohrerstown. Turn north on State 741, and at the intersection follow US 30 east to the exit for State 272 (Oregon Pike) north to Ephrata. From Ephrata, take US 322 west to Brickerville and State 501 south to Lititz and the intersection of US 30. The approximate total miles is sixty.

Every visit to Lancaster should begin with Central Market, the true heart of the city. A no-nonsense, solid brick building, Central has a long history dating back to 1730, when Andrew Hamilton, Lancaster's original city planner, set aside space for "erecting, keeping or holding" a market. In 1742 King George II of England established the site forever as a market, and in 1972 the U.S. Department of the Interior recognized the current structure as the oldest publicly owned, continually operated market in the United States by naming it a National Shrine.

And it is a shrine to gastronomy! Aisle after aisle is filled with the best that the rich central Pennsylvania farms produce. At Slaymaker's poultry stand, plump chickens clasp bouquets of parsley to their breasts. They are flanked by rows of hefty stewing hens, turkeys, Muscovy ducks, Cornish game hens, and skinned rabbits. Hodeckers Celery Farms stand sells nothing but their crisp golden blanched celery, and at Irwin S.Widders Produce, customers wait three deep for the crisp lettuce, ruddy tomatoes, slender zucchini, and verdant broccoli stacked on a shelf to form a green wall of florets. There are stands specializing in kettle-cooked potato chips; stands bursting with the vibrant colors of seasonal flowers; stands selling coffee, tea, and spices; deli stands with red pickled eggs, chowchow, apple butter, and watermelon pickles; and stands purveying everything from home-canned catsup to lye soap and quilts. Some Amish and Mennonites work the market, but there is a true variety of people of all ethnic backgrounds and religious persuasions.

After experiencing the sights and sounds of Central, walk a few steps to the Heritage Center Museum on Penn Square. The sage who said that good things come in small packages must have had in mind this collection of Lancaster County decorative and fine arts. Exhibits of quilts, samplers, furniture, silver, pewter, Pennsylvania long rifles, clocks, paintings, weather vanes, and folk art are well-explained and

Don't miss a visit to Central Market

strikingly displayed in the historic Old City Hall and Masonic Lodge. The museum's gift shop is an excellent source of contemporary folk art.

If you wish to further explore the city, the Historic Lancaster Walking Tour gives you the option of purchasing a comprehensive guidebook for self-guided excursions or enlisting the aid of a trained interpreter in colonial costume.

Although James Buchanan's home is within city limits, it is not easily accessible by foot. The elegant Federal residence of America's fifteenth president is set on four manicured acres and crowned with century-old trees. Maintained in the period of Buchanan's ownership from 1848 to 1868, the mansion was built in 1828 for a local lawyer and was purchased by Buchanan while he served as secretary of state to President James Polk.

Tours of Wheatlands are not casual self-guided strolls from room to room. Guides in period costume usher guests through a dozen chambers, including the Empire dining room where Buchanan entertained friends and political callers, the Victorian parlor where the president's niece Harriet Lane was married, and the study filled with original furnishings, books, and decorative objects. The circuit animates the life-style of a wealthy and politically advantaged man of the middle nineteenth century.

Leaving the city for rural Lancaster County, you recross busy US 30 and head for the country. The Landis Valley Museum is a collection of twenty-two buildings clustered around the crossroads of the small recreated village, which includes farmsteads and barns, a hotel and tavern, a country store, school, firehouse, visitors center, and tin, pottery, blacksmith, print, and leather-working shops. Dedicated to the preservation of Pennsylvania's rural past, the numerous exhibits and living history demonstrations interpret country life from colonial times through the end of the nineteenth century.

The museum began with a collecting passion that assumed heroic proportions. George and Henry Landis—good, solid Pennsylvania Germans whose ancestors had settled in Lancaster County in the early 1700s—recognized the significance of their people's history and culture and began accumulating objects from the 1700s and 1800s. By the 1920s their collection numbered more than 75,000 items, and they founded a small museum, which they housed on the grounds of their Landis Valley homestead. The state acquired the museum in 1953, and over the years it has grown from a handful of buildings to an impressive assemblage of original structures, relocated constructions, and new facilities.

The museum grounds are shaded by patriarchal trees, and in the gardens heirloom plants and flowers bloom. Old Dobbin neighs behind a rail fence, and cattle low in the pastures. During warm weather, costumed interpreters guide visitors through the village, and craftsmen recreate traditional skills such as weaving and blacksmithing. For children and adults, the Landis Valley Museum is both a bucolic idyll and a learning experience.

One of Lancaster's finest restaurants is on Rosehill Road, just three miles north of the museum via the Oregon Pike. The Log Cabin Restaurant was once a Prohibition speakeasy with illicit liquor hidden under the wooden booths. It still retains the outward appearances of a rural tavern, but the interior belies its rustic exterior with brass and crystal chandeliers, walls adorned with classic oil paintings, and crisp napery.

If you bypass an early dinner to press on to Ephrata, the Doneckers complex will minister to your needs at their elegant country French restaurant and four antique-filled bed and breakfasts: The Gerhart House, The Guesthouse, The Homestead, and the 1777 House. In the morning you may want to visit their 45,000-square-foot department store, which stocks creme de la crème fashions for men, women, children, and the home, or browse through the Artworks, the former Fleet Air shoe factory, which now serves as a permanent showcase for regional artists and craftsmen. A farmers' market adjoining the Artworks stocks everything from S. Clyde Weaver's delicious, smoky Lebanon bologna (a type of firm summer sausage) to The Amish Kitchen's Pennsylvania Dutch potpie.

The tranquility of early morning is an ideal time to visit Ephrata Cloister, one of America's earliest attempts at communal living. Founded in 1732 by Conrad Beissel, a German Pietist, the community of celibate brothers and sisters practiced an austere life-style and engaged in farming, fruit growing, basketry, papermaking, printing, book making, carpentry, and milling. A number of married householders lived off the Cloister grounds but worshiped there and supported the community's economy.

The Society's greatest contributions were in the fields of original choral music, calligraphy, and printing. Their reputation for charity was significant. Travelers were lodged and fed free of charge, and in 1777, after the Battle of Brandywine, 500 wounded soldiers were nursed back to health in buildings that had to be burned to prevent the spread of camp fever.

The Society declined after Beissel's death in 1768 due to lack of leadership, and by 1800 the celibate orders were practically extinct. In 1814 the remaining householders incorporated the Seventh Day German Baptist Church, which used the buildings until 1934; in 1941 the state took over the restoration and interpretation of the site.

Today's visitor will tour the grassy, tree-shaded grounds with a guide attired in the simple garb of a Society brother or sister. The Sister's House, or Saron, and the Meetinghouse, or Saal, are the most striking examples of the Rhenish architecture, but you'll also have the opportunity to see ten other sites, including a householder's residence, academy, Beissel

House, print shop, and bake house. Tarry a while in the graveyard among the mossy stones, and search out Beissel's final resting place.

Before leaving Ephrata, be sure to stop at Self Help Crafts of the World on Route 272, one block north of the hospital. Managed by the Mennonite Central Committee and dedicated to providing income to Third World craftspeople, the immense store stocks a cornucopia of gorgeous, sensibly priced handmade items ranging from rugs from Afghanistan to retablo story boxes from Peru. The tearoom is a popular lunch spot, with the menu featuring a different country each week.

Leaving Ephrata, you swing northwest through rolling farmland. Just 4.5 miles from the intersection of State 272 and US 322, Clearview Farm Bed and Breakfast provides a touch of elegance in a farm setting. The gracious limestone farmhouse has five guest rooms, each decorated in a different theme. The third-floor Lincoln and Washington rooms reveal the old original hand-pegged rafters, exposed stone walls, and authentic wide board flooring. Breakfast is a formal affair with a table set with fine china and crystal and featuring dishes such as ham and cheese soufflé accompanied by shoofly muffins or homemade raisin bread. The terrace sports a view of swans gliding over a modest pond and fertile Lancaster farmland stretching to the horizon.

South of Brickerville in Lititz, you won't find the Amish with their horse-drawn buggies but a tidy Moravian village dotted with greens, museums, and shops made for browsing—a tiny transplant of the culture that flourished in Bethlehem, Pennsylvania, and Winston-Salem, North Carolina.

On Moravian Square visit the Museum and Archives of the white-steepled Lititz Moravian Church. The collection of antique instruments reflects the strong role that music has traditionally played in the life of the congregation.

Directly behind the sanctuary, the cemetery, God's Acre, contains the graves of early church members and the last resting place of Gen. John Augustus Sutter of gold rush fame. A bitter and broke Sutter retired to Lititz and commuted to Washington to press vainly for government reparations in the destruction of his California property by miners.

To learn how to twist a pretzel and stock up on freshly baked twists, cross the street to the Julius Sturgis Pretzel House, birthplace of the American pretzel industry. The house, built in 1784, has been restored, and visitors can see pretzels being baked in the original 200-year-old brick ovens as well as in the modern plant.

Up the street, the Lititz Museum and adjoining Mueller House give visitors a glance at life in early Lititz, a time when all land was owned by the church and only members of the Moravian congregation could lease properties.

Large sections of East Main have been converted to shops and galleries. You won't want to miss Noah's Ark or the handworks [sic] for unusual gifts and handicrafts, H. B. Hardican Antiques, Judie's unusual women's clothing, and especially the Herb Shop, where you'll find more than 100 varieties of tea and coffee and more than 200 medicinal and culinary herbs. The profusion of goods from all points of the globe is almost overwhelming, but owner Barbara Zink and her knowledgeable staff are on hand to help you fill your needs.

That wonderful aroma drifting over town emanates from the Wilbur Chocolate Company, where you may buy confections such as Hershey Kiss look-alike Wilbur Buds or other confections. The Candy Americana Museum has displays of the candy-making process; a collection of 200 fine porcelain chocolate pots from manufacturers such as Sèvres, Haviland, and Dresden; and more than 1,000 varieties of molds, tins, boxes, and other candy memorabilia.

Lititz Springs Park, next to the chocolate factory, offers an opportunity to relax and unwind in a beautiful setting. Clear water bubbles out of the spring at the base of a hill, flows into a stone-walled retaining pond, and meanders in a channel under stone-arch footbridges to another retaining basin bordering Broad Street. Families picnic in the shade of old maples, sharing their leftovers with a vocal contingent of mallards who drift up and down the stream looking for handouts.

In the countryside outside of Lititz, Debbie and Werner Mosiman reinvent hospitality at their Swiss Woods Bed & Breakfast. Set on a wooded hillside overlooking Speedwell Lake, the commodious chalet is surrounded by flower beds bursting with color, and geranium-filled window boxes crown every sill.

The interior of the chalet is done in natural pine and oak, and the tall windows admit the maximum allotment of sunshine. The large common room, the Anker Stube, is dominated by a large sandstone fireplace surrounded by charming European-design furniture. Goose-down comforters supply toasty slumbers in the seven guest rooms, which are frequently occupied with overseas guests who feel right at home in the Continental atmosphere.

Breakfast is exceptional, with Debbie, a Lancaster county native, showcasing her culinary skills in what has to be one of the most bountiful tables in the area. In addition to goodies such as baked eggs and cheese, fresh muffins and croissants, and homemade jams, you're sure to find the luscious double-smoked bacon or savory ham for which Debbie's family, S. Clyde Weaver, is noted in farmers' markets throughout the region.

Before you return to the bustle of US 30, take a few minutes to stroll down to the lake. A great blue heron and American bittern fish in the shallows and a flock of Canada geese crop the tender shoots on the ranger's lawn. A solitary fisherman casts for bass. It's captivating, it's peaceful, it's Lancaster County.

In the Area

All numbers are within area code 717.

Central Market, Lancaster, 291-4740. Tuesday and Friday from 6:00 A.M. to 4:30 P.M.; Saturday from 6:00 A.M. to 2:00 P.M.

The Heritage Center Museum, Lancaster, 299-6440. May through November. Closed Monday.

Historic Lancaster Walking Tour, Lancaster, 392-1776. Daily from April through October, by appointment from November through March. Fee.

James Buchanan's Wheatlands, Lancaster, 392-8721. April 1 through November 30. Guided tours. Fee.

Landis Valley Museum, Lancaster, 569-0401. Closed Monday and holidays. Fee.

The Log Cabin Restaurant, Leola, 626-1181. Reservations required.

Doneckers Restaurant, Ephrata, 738-2421. Closed Wednesday and holidays.

Doneckers Guesthouse, 1777 House, The Gerhart House, and The Homestead, Ephrata, 733-8696.

Doneckers Artworks, Ephrata, 733-7900. Closed Wednesday.

Doneckers Fashion Store, Ephrata, 733-2231. Closed Wednesday and Sunday.

The Farmers' Market at Doneckers, Ephrata, 738-9555. Thursday through Saturday.

Ephrata Cloister, Ephrata, 733-6600. Daily. Fee.

Self Help Crafts of the World and Tearoom, Ephrata, 738-1101. Closed Sunday.

Clearview Farm Bed and Breakfast, Ephrata, 733-6333.

Julius Sturgis Pretzel House, Lititz, 626-4354. Closed Sunday. Fee.

The Mueller House and Lititz Museum, Lititz Historical Foundation, Lititz, 627-4636. Monday through Saturday. Museum self-guided; Mueller House tour. Fee.

Lititz Moravian Church and Museum and Archives, Lititz, 626-8515 or 626-4275. Saturday afternoons from Memorial Day through September. Off season, call for appointment.

Noah's Ark, Lititz, 627-0464. Closed Sunday.

Landworks, Lititz, 627-4545. Closed Sunday.

H. B. Hardican Antiques, Lititz, 627-4603. Closed Sunday.

Judie, Lititz, 627-4949. Closed Sunday.

The Herb Shop, Lititz, 626-9206. Closed Sunday.

Wilbur's Candy Americana Museum and Factory Candy Outlet, Lititz, 626-0967. Closed Sunday.

Swiss Woods Bed & Breakfast, Lititz, 800-594-8018 or 627-3358.

Pennsylvania Dutch Convention & Visitors Bureau, Lancaster, 800-735-2629 or 299-8901.

6 ~

Paths of War

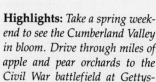

Getting there: Take the Pennsylvania Turnpike to Carlisle.

Highlights: *Take a spring weekend to see the Cumberland Valley in bloom. Drive through miles of apple and pear orchards to the Civil War battlefield at Gettysburg, "High Water Mark of the Confederacy." Go antiquing in New Oxford and Carlisle. Visit the site of the famed Carlisle Indian School. Wander out to Boiling Springs, where you can cast for trout in the Yellow Breeches or merely relax by the pristine lake.*

The Route

From the Pennsylvania Turnpike Carlisle exit 16, take US 11 west to Carlisle. From the square, join State 641 east, bear right on State 74 south, pass under I-81, and turn south on Forge Road, SR 2003, for Boiling Springs.

From the center of town, follow State 174 west to State 34 south, through Mount Holly Springs, Idaville, and Biglerville to Gettysburg.

Leaving Gettysburg, take US 30 east to New Oxford. Leaving New Oxford, continue on US 30 to State 94 north through York Springs to the outskirts of Mount Holly, where you follow State 34 north to I-81, exit 14. The approximate total miles is sixty-six.

The Great Valley sweeps across south central Pennsylvania and joins the Shenandoah Valley in Virginia. In the early days, settlers traversed the length of "Mother Cumberland" to new lands in the west. A natural corridor, the valley saw the movement of hostile armies up and down its length from the French and Indian to the Civil wars.

Today's valley holds the echoes of former times. As you arrive in Carlisle, you pass the gates of the Carlisle Barracks, since 1951 home of the U.S. Army War College, established by Elihu Root, secretary of war in McKinley's cabinet, "not to promote war, but to preserve peace by adequate preparation to repel aggression."

The second oldest army post in the United States, Carlisle was founded by Col. John Stanwix of the British Army in 1757 and during the Revolution served as an ordnance center for Gen. George Washington. The barracks is perhaps best known as the site of the Carlisle Indian School.

In the years of the school's existence, from 1879 to 1918, students from eighty-seven tribes from all parts of the United States learned academic and vocational skills. Under Coach Pop Warner, the sports program honed the natural talents of legends such as Jim Thorpe, "the greatest athlete who ever lived"; Louis Tewanima, second in the 5,000- and 10,000-meter runs in the 1912 Olympics; and Chief Bender, a Philadelphia baseball pitcher.

Carlisle is an open post, and if you show identification at the guard station, the soldier on duty will admit you and provide you with a map. Little of the Indian School remains today—only the sad graveyard at the rear of the post. Many children died while at Carlisle, most of "black measles." If you visit the cemetery, you can read their names: "Dora, daughter of Brave Bull," "Simon Dakosu, Apache," "Ernest, Son of Chief White Thunder." They lie beneath Cumberland soil far from their reservation homes.

Another post relic of a former era is the Hessian Powder Magazine, constructed in 1777 by Hessian prisoners after their capture by Washington at the Battle of Trenton. The magazine, once used for storage of gunpowder, cannon shot, and small arms, is now a museum tracing the barrack's history from the colonial period through its conversion into an educational institute.

Just down the street from the post's main gate, you come to the first evidence of Carlisle as an antique-hunters' mecca. Northgate 1 and Northgate 2 frame both sides of North Hanover Street with a total of 200 dealers. There is something for every collector in these cooperatives, from Victorian jewelry to old stoneware jugs.

Downtown Carlisle sports a dozen antique shops, with dealers tenanting the old jewelry store, drugstore, and the like. Downtown Antiques is a multidealer co-op with an across-the-board selection on two floors; Antiques World has an especially nice variety of depression glass; and Antiques on Hanover has a high-quality collection of furniture, ranging from Federal through Victorian and into the twentieth century. Noll & Reinhold always stocks an assortment of old quilts in addition to their specialty—old photographs, daguerreotypes, and tintypes.

The Carlisle Fairgrounds hosts Spring Antiques at Carlisle and Autumn Antiques at Carlisle, two-day spectaculars held the third weekend of May and September. More than 1,100 dealers from all over the country drum their wares in the open and under roof.

If all this browsing has left you with an appetite, drop in at the California Cafe at 52 West Pomfret. Thomas Hall and Oliver Hazan have created an intimate bistro with a cuisine suggestive of French family dining. The fixed-price, four-course dinners might include entrées such as chicken in sour cream with paprika and mushrooms, fresh tuna steak with béarnaise sauce, and flounder almondine. The lunch menu lists creamy quiche, homemade soups, sandwiches, and innovative hot entrées.

The campuses of Dickinson College and Dickinson School of Law are within walking distance of the cafe, as is the Old Graveyard off East South Street. The sturdy limestone wall marks the burial site of Molly Pitcher, the heroine of the Revolutionary War battle of Monmouth. If you remember your history, her real name was Mary Ludwig Hays. During the hostilities, she brought pitchers of water to colonials wounded in the field, and when her husband was injured, she took his place at the cannon battery. It is said that General Washington thanked her personally after the conflict. Her resting place is marked with a life-size statue of the heroine, ramrod in hand.

From Carlisle, it is just four miles to Boiling Springs, a nineteenth-century village of undeniable charm, with old limestone buildings, sheltering shade trees, and a seven-acre lake, its surface marked by the active boil of more than thirty springs rising from limestone caverns 1,800 feet below the surface. With a constant year-round temperature of fifty-three degrees, the lake is a never-freezing magnet for a variety of waterfowl, ranging from common mallards to more unusual varieties such as pintails and canvasbacks. Children come with sacks of bread to feed the chubby flock, drawing gaggles of honking, quacking, competing freeloaders. Spring is especially winsome, with small fluffy babies bobbing like feathered corks, learning the ropes from their parents.

Boiling Springs was once the site of a Revolutionary War iron furnace, which produced cannon and shot for Washington's army. The old furnace has been stabilized and can still be seen on the banks of Yellow Breeches Creek, one of the East's prime trout streams. On any day during the season, you will find fishermen casting for brookies, browns, or rainbows in the "catch and release" waters. At Yellow Breeches Outfitters across from the post office, Bill Zeiders caters to these Izaak Waltons with a full line of fly-fishing tackle, a guide service, and necessities such as waders and fishing vests.

The Mid-Atlantic Office of the Appalachian Trail Conference is next door, and if you've a hankering to try your hand at a moderate hike, they will point you in the direction of South Mountain and the six-mile stretch between the town and Whiskey Springs. It's one of the nicest walks in the area, with impressive views from the ridge and interesting and varied geology.

If your ambitions are less elevated, you might want to take a self-guided walking tour of the town. For a brochure detailing architecture and thumbnail historical sketches, stop in at the CCNB bank office next to the post office and request the brochure prepared by the civic association.

Once you've walked or hiked, you're likely to appreciate a swim. The Boiling Springs Pools are a landmark, built in 1927 and in use ever since. The four pools have varying depths and may be enjoyed by everyone from the wading toddler to the expert swimmer.

In the early 1900s the town had a trolley line connecting it to nearby boroughs and to an amusement park with a dance pavilion, picnic grove, and carousel. The park is gone, but the stone hotel lives on as the Boiling Springs Tavern, recognized as one of the finest dining spots in Cumberland County. Geoff and Debi Keith serve contemporary American cuisine with a constantly changing range of blackboard specials. With an emphasis on lighter meals, the menu leans heavily to seafood specialties prepared to be easy on the waistline, but your good intentions may vanish when you're tempted with their selection of luscious desserts.

For such a small village, Boiling Springs has a variety of accommodations. On a rise above the lake, Highland House has responded to the tender ministrations of Barry and Michaela Buchter, and the old Ege estate has been transformed into an urbane bed and breakfast. The 1776 two-and-a-half-story Federal ironmaster's mansion once played host to Robert Morris and John Hancock. Rumor has it that Baron William Henry Steigel, one of the first colonial glassmakers and a frequent guest, is buried on the front lawn.

Across the lake on Front Street, John and Molly Garman's Second Empire–style house was built in the 1860s by Daniel Kaufman, the village planner. Out of fourteen rooms, they have carved a cozy four-room second-floor lair for bed and breakfasters.

Finally, just up the road from the center of town, Allenberry Resort Inn and Playhouse occupies land once part of a 1685 William Penn land grant and owned for a while by relatives of Davy Crockett, the legendary frontiersman. Today Allenberry is a cloistered retreat with several restaurants, a variety of accommodations, tennis courts, a swimming pool, and a professional theater. Located directly on the Yellow Breeches, the resort's shaded grounds and old limestone buildings are popular with anglers as well as vacationers.

Leaving Boiling Springs, you head south, passing the old section of Craigshead, with its collection of pierced-sided brick bank barns and fine old farms. State 34 takes you up the rise toward Mount Holly Springs. Howard Miller, one of the area's most respected and knowledgeable antique dealers, has his shop in back of the limestone house on the hill with the blue shutters. With an inventory topping 10,000 items, Miller carries a broad general line in addition to specializing in lamps, lighting devices, and clocks.

A short distance from Mount Holly, you pass through Michaux State Forest and into Adams County, with its rolling hills spring-dappled in pink and white apple blossoms. The colorful patchwork resembles a primitive by Grandma Moses.

Gettysburg is a busy tourist town, with all the attendant advantages—a selection of restaurants and accommodations—and some of the disadvantages, such as prime-time crowds. Beneath all the hoopla, a very basic attraction is the National Military Park, looking much the same today as it did in the Civil War during those decisive three days of July 1863, when the forces of Confederate Gen. Robert E. Lee were overwhelmed by Union troops commanded by Gen. George G. Meade.

Gettysburg is not a place to experience from the window of a car or trailing behind a hoard of tourists. Try to time your visit on a weekday, and early morning is best. April and May, with cooler weather and lack of crowds, are ideal, and you have the bonus of seeing the dogwood and redbud in full bloom.

Before you set out, stop at the visitors center for an orientation to the park. The electric map display is extremely helpful in visualizing the troop movements. Then get out and walk, experiencing the battlefield as the soldiers once did. The High Water Mark Trail leads past regimental monuments, part of an artillery battery, General Meade's headquarters, and the point where Union troops repulsed Pickett's charge. There are other alternatives, including short hikes to Devil's Den, where Confederate sharpshooters fired on Union soldiers at Little Roundtop, or Point of Woods, where Lee acknowledged defeat.

No visitor to Gettysburg should miss the National Cemetery, where on November 19, 1863, President Abraham Lincoln gave his brief two-minute address, which has gone down in history as one of the most eloquent speeches in the English language. If you are lucky enough to visit during the November 19th celebration, you will hear Jim Getty recite the

Memorials at Gettysburg

address. Getty, who every evening portrays Lincoln at the Conflict Theater, is immensely moving as the sixteenth president.

If you'd like to visit the Eisenhower National Historic Site, where Ike and Mamie spent their retirement, check in as soon as possible at the tour information desk in the visitors center. The 189 acres, with bank barn, guest house, and modified Georgian main house, may be viewed from the observation tower off West Confederate Avenue, but if you wish to tour the property, you must travel by shuttle. Only a limited number of visitors per day are permitted, and tickets are on a first-come, first-served basis.

Gettysburg has an assortment of eateries, from diners to haute cuisine. Two of the best are Polly and Allison Giles's Blue Parrot Bistro, with eclectic decor and American contemporary fare, and the 1776 Dobbin House Tavern, with traditional provender, in-house spring room, and minimuseum of site-related artifacts.

Leaving Gettysburg, you take the Lincoln Highway to New Oxford, "the little town with the beautiful circle." The village boosters glorify the square with its jetted fountain, but most visitors remember it as the quaint town with a profusion of antique outlets. New Oxford Antique Mall on West Golden Lane has sixty-six dealers, with a mix of antiques and collectibles; the New Oxford Antique Center has forty dealers highlighting Pennsylvania furniture and accessories. Add some two dozen or more independent dealers to the mix, and you have an antique lovers' bonanza, which swells even further during the annual Antique Market on the third Saturday in June.

There are a couple of places dealing in old model trains, one or two stocking old wicker, and even a dealer in antique Irish furniture. If Ryland Robinson is sitting in at Lor-Ing Creations—a shop owned by his wife, Lorraine, and Ingrid

Luckenbaugh—stop and chat. He has lived in the town all his life, has worked in the trade since his teenage years, and knows the local ins and outs as well as most and better than some.

From New Oxford, you head north again, back into upper Adams County. If you're looking for a place to stay, you needn't search any farther than Goose Chase Farm on Blueberry Road near York Springs. This restored eighteenth-century stone house with its manicured twenty-five acres is set on a pond, down a dirt road, in the heart of the orchard country. Owners Marsha and Rich Lucidi are the ideal hosts, attentive but not intrusive. Marsha, garbed in Colonial attire, serves a big country breakfast; Rich tackles the grounds, works in the gardens, and tends his hillside vineyard. The atmosphere is so relaxing that guests with plans to sightsee often spend their weekends lazing by the pool or reading on the deck in the company of Morgan and Garrett, the Lucidi's mellow chocolate labs.

The lovely old house has a sunny dining room and spacious living room decorated in Williamsburg wine and celadon, with a damask camelback sofa, wing chairs in flame stitch, shelves of books, and bibelots collected from all over the globe. The main house has three attractive guest rooms, but the ultimate in privacy and luxury are the two carriage house suites with working fireplaces.

As a souvenir of your sojourn, stop for fresh fruit at Peters Orchards between York Springs and Mount Holly. They have apples all year long, and spring ushers in crops of tender asparagus and succulent red strawberries. Their canned peaches, plums, and pears are nonpareil, and they stock a wide selection of their own jams and jellies, apple butter, and honey.

In the Area

All numbers are within area code 717 unless otherwise indicated.

Carlisle Barracks, Carlisle, 245-3131. Hessian Powder Magazine Museum, Saturday and Sunday.

Northgate 1 & 2, Carlisle, 243-9744 and 243-5802.

Downtown Antiques, Carlisle, 249-0395.

Antiques World, Carlisle, 245-2528.

Antiques on Hanover, Carlisle, 249-6285.

Noll & Reinhold Antiques, Carlisle, 249-0946.

Antiques at Carlisle, Carlisle Fairgrounds, Carlisle, 243-7855.

California Cafe, Carlisle, 249-2028. Closed Sunday and Monday.

Yellow Breeches Outfitters, Boiling Springs, 258-6752.

Mid-Atlantic Office, Appalachian Trail Conference, Boiling Springs, 258-5771. Irregular hours.

Boiling Springs Pools, Boiling Springs, 258-6169. Memorial Day through Labor Day.

Boiling Springs Tavern, Boiling Springs, 258-3614. Closed Sunday and Monday.

Highland House, Boiling Springs, 258-3744.

The Garmanhaus, Boiling Springs, 258-3980.

Allenberry Resort Inn and Playhouse, Boiling Springs, 258-3211. Closed from mid-November through April 1.

Howard Miller Antiques, Mount Holly Springs, 486-3652.

Gettysburg National Military Park, Gettysburg, 334-1124.

The Conflict Theater and Bookshop, Gettysburg, 337-1728.

Dobbin House Tavern, Gettysburg, 334-2100.

The Blue Parrot Bistro, Gettysburg, 337-3739. Closed Sunday and Monday.

Lor-Ing Creations, New Oxford, 624-7939. Closed Monday.

Goose Chase' Gardeners, 528-8877.

Peters Orchards, York Springs, 528-4380.

Cumberland Valley Visitors Center (Carlisle and Cumberland County Antique Dealers), Carlisle, 249-4801.

Harrisburg-Hershey-Carlisle Tourism & Convention Bureau (Carlisle & Boiling Springs), Harrisburg, 800-995-0969 or 232-1377.

Gettysburg Travel Council, Inc., Gettysburg, 334-6274.

New Oxford Area Chamber of Commerce (antique shop listing), P.O. Box 152, New Oxford, PA 17350. No phone.

7 ~

Valleys of the Susquehanna

Getting there: Take I-80 to exit 30 to US 15 south to Lewisburg.

Highlights: *Take two or three days to visit Lewisburg, home of Bucknell University, and drive the Amish back country to State College and the campus of Penn State. Stop at the Victorian town of Bellefonte, Fisherman's Paradise, and Boalsburg, where Memorial Day was born. Check out the quilts and Buggy Museum in Mifflinburg, stop for goodies at Walnut Acres farm and store, and finish with a memorable ride across the Susquehanna on the old-time Millersburg Ferry.*

The Route

Leave I-80 at exit 30, just west of the Susquehanna River, and take US 15 south to Lewisburg. Connect with State 192 west for approximately forty-five miles and turn west on State 144 in Centre Hall. Proceed to Bellefonte, where you turn west on State 144/150 to Milesburg and east on State 150 for 2.5 miles to the turnoff to Curtin Village. Return west on State 150 and east on State 144/150. In Bellefonte join State 550 east and State 26 west to State College.

Leaving State College, rejoin State 26 west to Shingle-
town Road (State 45). Turn north and stay on State 45 through
Boalsburg and an additional forty-two miles to Mifflinburg.
West of the business district, turn east on State 104 and drive
twenty-two miles through Penns Creek and Middleburg.
Rejoin US 15 north of Liverpool and continue south to Harrisburg via the Millersburg Ferry or US 22/322 and the Clarks
Ferry bridge over the Susquehanna. The approximate total
miles is 180.

Although thousands beat a path to Beaver Stadium to
watch Penn State's Nittany Lions play football under the leadership of the legendary Joe Paterno, not too many take time to
discover the pleasures of the back roads linking State College
with surrounding Susquehanna Valley villages.

Your trip begins east of State College with another university town. Lewisburg is home of Bucknell College, a four-year
liberal arts school founded in 1846. Situated on a hill overlooking the town, Bucknell's beautiful 300-acre campus incorpo-
rates a feeling of scholarly containment. With a student body
of slightly more than 3,200, it is considerably smaller than its
neighbor to the west.

Lewisburg itself is a well-preserved historic town, and a
walk down Market Street reveals many examples of the beautiful Federal style of architecture so popular before the Civil
War. These buildings were spared from destruction by a slow
area economy from the 1930s through the 1950s. During those
years there was little money for modernization or expansion,
and unless a structure was irreparably damaged by fire or
an act of God, residents preserved what their forefathers
had built.

This did not apply to the lares and penates, which were
more readily turned into cash. In 1936 one area native
returned to her hometown with her wealthy, retired husband
and was horrified to see so many of the locality's ethnic German decorative arts disappearing into the antique markets of

New York and Philadelphia. Edith and John Fetherston decided to stem this tide, and after purchasing three adjoining townhouses on Water Street, they renovated the buildings with the objective of establishing both a residence and museum, which would act as a repository of Susquehanna Valley decorative arts. They named their museum Packwood House, after John's ancestral home in England, and used their considerable funds to rescue the works of early area craftsmen.

Of the museum's twenty-seven rooms, twenty are on the docent-guided tours, which are tailored to the interests of individuals or groups. Visitors will discover extensive collections of nineteenth-century painted furniture, local stoneware and redware, Victorian glassware, and textiles, including many signed and documented quilts. Edith was a talented amateur painter, and she hung her own works lavishly, including her "rooster" series, which won her considerable acclaim.

Across town, the Slifer House Museum exposes another facet of Lewisburg's history. Built in 1860 by Eli Slifer, Pennsylvania Governor Andrew Gregg Curtin's secretary of state, the twenty-room mansion was designed by Philadelphia architect Samuel Sloan and was featured in the 1862 *Godey's Lady's Book*. Sold to Dr. Lamont Ross after Slifer's death, the property passed to the Evangelical Association in 1915; from that date until 1975 it functioned as the United Methodist Home. It was rescued from the wrecking ball by concerned local citizens, who since 1976 have been working to restore the home to its Victorian splendor.

The first floor is 90 percent complete, with parlor, sitting room or library, dining room, and kitchen furnished in period furniture and accessories. Special collections include a doctor's office, complete with early medical tools, and an assembly of musical instruments, ranging from an 1846 melodeon to an 1890's Virginia music box—all in working condition.

Lewisburg has several top-quality bed and breakfast establishments. The Pineapple Inn on Market Street is housed in an 1857 Federal home designed by Louis Palmer, a noted state architect. The cozy guest rooms and formal parlor are antique decorated, and innkeeper Charles North tempts guests with breakfasts incorporating fresh Amish breads, eggs, and meats, and tasty natural granola from nearby Walnut Acres organic farms.

If you prefer a more bucolic ambience, the Inn on Fiddler's Tract fills the bill. The intriguing name comes from the original 1,610 acres that were deeded to an itinerant fiddler in 1780 by John Penn, son of the state's founder. The inn has five elegant suites and beautiful gardens graced by a gazebo and fish pond. Natalie and Tony Boldurian have transformed the historic limestone building on thirty-three acres into a relaxing getaway for the overstressed.

For a quick, informal meal, Bechtel's Dairy and Restaurant has been serving customers since 1923 with homemade specials and thirty-eight flavors of their own ice cream. For a more elegant meal, you won't go wrong with the Lewisburg Inn on Market Street.

Antique lovers should check out the Lewisburg Roller Mills Marketplace, with ninety dealers housed in a restored 1883 mill building on Saint Mary Street. There are two floors of collectibles, a glass showcase gallery, a craft room, and the Little Red Hen Restaurant, which specializes in homemade soups and pies.

Leaving town on State 192, turn right on Hoffa Mill Road, a mile or two beyond the Inn on Fiddler's Tract. Down a twisting country lane you'll find Grove's Mill, a working roller mill running solely on water power. Built in 1774, the native stone and brick building on Buffalo Creek has been in the Grove family since 1910. Today Charles and Bessie Grove operate the mill as a full-service feed and supply, meeting the needs of the agricultural community in addition to stone-grinding a variety of flours. Home bakers buying roasted cornmeal or pastry and bread flour mingle with farmers picking up sacks of all-purpose mash for chickens.

Retracing your steps back to State 192 and turning westward, you travel through the fields and farms of Buffalo Valley before climbing out of the lowlands and passing through the hemlock and white pine forests and rhododendron thickets of Bald Eagle State Forest.

Descending into Brush Valley at Livonia, you pass through fertile farmland shared by the Amish and their non-Amish, or "English," neighbors. In the small village of Madisonburg you can stop at the Madisonburg Bake Shop, where Eli and Katie Stoltzfus turn out Penn Dutch treats such as wet bottom shoofly pies, sticky buns, egg noodles, and a variety of cookies, including the ever-popular whoopie pies— yo-yo–shaped sweets with gooey vanilla filling sandwiched between two cakelike chocolate rounds. Across the street, Fisher's Harness & Shoe Shop sells everything from horse bits to buggy whips, along with a full line of shoes and boots— some for every day and some "chust for nice."

Five miles east of Centre Hall is Penn's Cave, the nation's only all-water cavern viewed entirely by boat. Even if you're not much of a cave buff, you'll enjoy the leisurely ride in the red barges as they make the mile-long traverse of the limestone cavern, exit for a turn around Lake Nittany—the headwaters of Penn's Creek—and return through the cave. Like any respectable cavern, there is a legend—of Indian princess Nitanee and her French trapper lover, Malachi Boyer. Unable to marry because of Indian custom, they ran away but were captured, and Malachi was thrown into Penn's Cave to die. On moonless nights, they say, he can still be heard calling "Nitanee, Nitanee." It's wonderful nonsense, but the cavern is beautiful, and there is a wildlife sanctuary with white-tailed deer, wild turkey, and Boomer, a North American mountain lion and the living symbol of Penn State's famous mascot.

Reaching Centre Hall, you'll want to stop at Sweet Annie Herbs on South Pennsylvania Avenue. Ann Marie Wishard is a wizard with growing things, and her knowledge of herbs is encyclopedic. She has nostrums for arthritis, insomnia, and headaches. She has potions to smooth the skin or de-flea your dog. Needless to say, she stocks every culinary herb from allspice to thyme. Her shop is a wonderful place to browse, have a cup of herbal tea, and relax.

If you're beginning to crave nourishment, at the Whistle Stop Restaurant in the old Centre Hall railroad depot, Dick Fuller and his crew serve three meals a day in rail-motif dining rooms. The menu is traditional, with favorites such as crab cakes and chicken and waffles. With the exception of yeast breads, everything is made on the premises, including the stock base for the daily soup specials.

State 144 from Centre Hall will take you into Bellefonte, whose claim to fame rests in its impressive Victorian architecture and its prominence as the birthplace of seven state governors. The town clings to a steep hillside, and roller coaster lanes run between the heights and Spring Creek. A historical walking tour begins at the old train station and accesses the most outstanding Bellefonte structures, including the Hastings Mansion, home of Governor Daniel H. Hastings, and the Tuscan Revival residence of Governor Curtin. Don't miss Big Spring, the city's water supply and the origin of the town's name after being viewed by French statesman Talleyrand, who proclaimed it a "belle fonte," or beautiful spring. The town park and sculpture garden are named in Tallyrand's honor.

From the town's earliest history, its economy and that of the environs centered around iron works. A detour to Curtin Village is worth your time if you want to catch a glimpse of an

The mill at Curtain Village

iron plantation in the 1800s, including a handsome 1831 stuccoed stone mansion restored to its pre-Victorian–Empire style. The nine-room residence occupied by ironmaster Roland Curtin and his extended family of eighteen has an imposing entrance hall and center stairway, a parlor with twelve-foot ceilings, two sitting rooms, four bedrooms, and a functional kitchen.

The ironworks includes a charcoal-fired, cold-air blast furnace, which is a reconstruction of Pleasant Furnace, built in 1848 to replace the original fire-ravaged Eagle Furnace. The site is owned by the state Historical and Museum Commission but is managed by the volunteers of the Roland Curtin Foundation, who do yeoman's duty maintaining the property and giving tours.

On your way back through Bellefonte, you might stop for lunch or dinner at The Gamble Mill Tavern, the town's first building to be placed on the National Register of Historic Places. Originally a rolling mill manufacturing flour and feed, the three-story brick mill on the banks of Spring Creek was saved from demolition in 1975 and transformed into a handsome restaurant serving some of the finest cuisine in the area.

Anglers and children of all ages will love Fisherman's Paradise and adjoining Bellefonte Hatchery, just out of town off State 150. The hatchery has display ponds of large palomino, brown, brook, and rainbow trout; and the cultivation pens are a-squirm with hatchlings of all sizes. Spring Creek, which flows by the property, is a limestone stream with a number of trophy-size fish—an irresistible attraction to many aspiring Izaak Waltons.

State College is home to America's second-oldest land grant institution. Penn State University was founded as the Farmers' High School in 1855, and became the Agricultural

College of Pennsylvania in 1862, the Pennsylvania State College in 1874, and Pennsylvania State University in 1953.

With more than 40,000 full-time students in residence on campus, State College bustles with activity, and parking can be at a premium. Other than strolling the grounds, visiting the Nittany Lion "Shrine," and hobnobbing with students and professors at various watering holes and cafes, you can be both amused and educated by taking advantage of the school's museums and cultural events.

The Matson Museum of Anthropology on the second floor of the Carpenter Building contains a collection illustrating the wide range of human cultural and biological diversity. A model Mesoamerican pole and thatch farmhouse is featured in one area; another section displays fossil skulls from *Australopithecus africanus* to modern *Homo sapiens.*

The Earth and Mineral Sciences Museum in the Steidle Building has special darkened rooms displaying both fluorescent and luminescent minerals; a vast collection of mineral industry paintings; a presentation of minerals used in painting, such as raw sienna and ocher; and case after case of crystals and semiprecious minerals, both in their natural state and faceted for gem wear. Perhaps the most popular display is the rendition in glass replicas of the world's most famous diamonds, including the Jonker and Kohinoor.

Other options include inspecting the insect world at the Frost Entomological Museum or visiting the Palmer Museum of Art and Zoller Gallery, the Paul Robeson Cultural Center, the National Cable Television Center and Museum, or the Football Hall of Fame, featuring memorabilia from the university's gridiron history.

An obligatory stop before leaving campus is the Creamery, where you can purchase ice cream made from the rich milk of Penn State's own dairy herd. Ben and Jerry, the Vermont ice cream moguls, got their start with a Penn State course, and after a cone at the Creamery, you will know where they got their inspiration.

Accommodations in and near State College are diverse, running from bed and breakfasts to chain motels. Two of the best are the elegant Nittany Lion Inn on West Park Avenue, and the Split Pine Farmhouse in nearby Pine Grove Mills. The Inn has always enjoyed a good reputation with State College visitors, and with a new addition and the refurbishing of existing space, it is more gracious than ever.

If you prefer a more intimate atmosphere, Mae McQuade's Split Pine Farmhouse will appeal. The spacious Federal-style building houses a felicitous combination of American antiques and bibelots collected from forty-five years of travel as a military wife. Mae has a special way with breakfasts, and your meal may include delicacies such as Mushrooms Charlotte with currant sauce, popovers, and champagne granita.

Heading east on State 45, you pass the outskirts of Boalsburg, where Memorial Day began in 1864 when Emma Hunter and Sophie Hall went to the local cemetery to decorate the graves of all the soldiers buried there. Five years later Congress passed the ordinance designating May 30 as a day to commemorate America's veterans.

The village of Boalsburg is a short distance off the highway. With its open square, early log and stone homes, and main street lined with shops and eateries, it is a pleasant place to browse away an hour or an afternoon.

On the village edge, the Columbus Chapel and Boal Mansion Museum is our country's strongest link to the Italian explorer. The chapel was part of the Columbus family castle in Spain; after it was inherited by descendants of Columbus in the Boal family, it was disassembled and brought to Pennsylvania, where it was housed in a stone building constructed to contain it. Chapel artifacts include Columbus's own admiralty desk and one of his explorer's crosses.

The mansion has been home since 1789 to nine generations of the Boal family. It contains room after room of priceless furnishings, all left the way they were when the last Boal lived there in 1992. The building's time-worn exterior proclaims a need for renovation, but for anyone who can look past peeling paint, the Boal Mansion is a treasure trove.

Off Boal Avenue the Pennsylvania Military Museum examines the state's martial history, spanning the time from Benjamin Franklin's first unit, "The Associators," to the Gulf War. Highlight of the museum is a walk through a World War I battlefield, complete with old vehicles, foxholes, sound and light effects, and voices of the medical evacuation squad. The sixty-five-acre park surrounding the museum features equipment, memorials, and monuments including the 28th Division Shrine.

Leaving Boalsburg, State 45 eastward takes you through terrain similar to your initial area approach on State 192 (the roads parallel each other). When you once again reach the Buffalo Valley, you might enjoy stopping in Hartleton at the Country Store, where bulk lots of staples are sold and Amish women bake bread, pies, and cookies every day.

Before joining State 104 west of Mifflinburg, take time to drive into town. A century ago Mifflinburg was known as the "buggy town," and its entire economy was geared to carriage building. The Mifflinburg Buggy Museum gives a nod to that prosperous era, preserving the William A. Heiss Coach Works with its shop, repository, and house. The repository, or showroom, houses a variety of locally made vehicles, and the shop contains the blacksmith, wood, paint, and stitching departments with the original forge and tools. The home is restored to reflect the furnishings of a family of modest means.

If you covet handmade quilts, stop in at Mary Koons Amish Quilts on Chestnut. The diminutive Mary stocks hand-stitched quilts made by the central Pennsylvania Amish, Mennonite, and talented "English" women, in addition to needlework supplies, quilted wall hangings, pillows, aprons, and throws.

On the 500 block of Chestnut, Joannah Purnell Skucek's Design Tiles studio and showroom features hand-shaped and hand-painted ceramic tiles. Her early American butterprint tile collection is one of her most popular lines, but she will design any specialty tile to a client's need, or duplicate an existing design.

Three miles south of Mifflinburg, Bill Lynch's Penns Creek Pottery is located in a comely old mill nestled on the banks of Penns Creek. Built in 1818, the mill is a gallery for not only Bill's handsome utilitarian stoneware but also the works of other quality craftspeople.

Up the hill from the mill, the dogleg turnoff to Walnut Acres takes you along a cow pasture, beside a stream, and finally to one of the oldest organic farms in the country. Founded in 1946 by Paul and Betty Keene with a commitment to providing the purest, most wholesome food possible, Walnut Acres puts into practice what its founders had learned at an organic farming school near Philadelphia. The years passed with three generations of Keenes living and working the land. Catalog sales of their products have skyrocketed, taking their organic foods to every state in the union and to several foreign countries as well.

A visit to the farm provides a heartwarming look into a business built on an ideal. Weekdays, there are tours of the plant where you can watch the staff grind peanut butter from whole red-skinned goobers or can a batch of field-ripened tomatoes. You can walk the grounds, have a picnic, or visit the farm store for a bite of lunch, a pantry restocking, or a browse through their extensive book section.

Approximately thirteen miles beyond the village of Penns Creek, State 104 rejoins US 15. To reach Harrisburg you may access US 22/322 and cross the Clarks Ferry bridge, or head south to Liverpool, where you can cross the Susquehanna on the Millersburg Ferry, the only wooden stern-wheel ferry in operation in America. The service is daily from dawn to dark except during the winter freeze-up.

In the Area

All telephone numbers are within area code 717 unless otherwise indicated.

The Packwood House Museum, Lewisburg, 524-0323. Closed Monday. Fee.

Slifer House Museum, Lewisburg, 524-2271. Tuesday through Friday afternoons; Monday and weekends by appointment. Fee.

The Pineapple Inn, Lewisburg, 524-6200.

The Inn on Fiddler's Tract, Lewisburg, 523-7197.

Bechtel's Dairy and Restaurant, Lewisburg, 524-2229.

The Lewisburg Inn, Lewisburg, 523-8200. Thursday through Saturday evenings.

Lewisburg Roller Mills Marketplace, Lewisburg, 524-5733.

Grove's Mill, Lewisburg, 524-2436. Monday through Friday.

Madisonburg Bake Shop, Madisonburg, no phone. Wednesday through Saturday. Closed in January.

Fisher's Harness & Shoe Shop, Madisonburg, no phone. Closed Sunday.

Penn's Cave, Centre Hall, 814-364-1664. Daily from January through November; weekends only in December. Fee.

Sweet Annie Herbs, Centre Hall, 814-364-1206.

The Whistle Stop Restaurant, Centre Hall, 814-364-2544.

Bellefonte Chamber of Commerce, Train Station, Bellefonte, map of historical walking tour), 814-355-2917. Monday through Friday. Map available weekends at Boscaino's Variety Store, across from the Train Station.

Curtin Village, Bellefonte, 814-355-1982. Wednesday through Sunday from Memorial Day through Labor Day. Fee.

The Gamble Mill Tavern, Bellefonte, 814-355-7764. Closed Sunday.

Fisherman's Paradise and Bellefonte Hatchery, Bellefonte, 814-355-3371.

Pennsylvania State University, State College. Map available in any parking kiosk on campus.

Matson Museum of Anthropology, State College, 814-865-3853 .

Penn State Earth and Mineral Sciences Museum and Art Gallery, State College, 814-865-6427. Monday through Friday.

The University Creamery, State College, 814-865-7535.

Nittany Lion Inn, State College, 800-233-7505.

Split Pine Farmhouse Bed & Breakfast, Pine Grove Mills, 814-238-2028.

Pennsylvania Military Museum, Boalsburg, 814-466-6263. Closed Monday.

Columbus Chapel and Boal Mansion Museum, Boalsburg, 814-466-6210. May 1 through October 31. Closed Tuesday.

Hartleton's Country Store, Hartleton, 922-1222. Closed Sunday.

Mifflinburg Buggy Museum, Mifflinburg, 966-4849. Tuesday through Sunday from May through mid-September. Fee.

Mary Koons Amish Quilts, Mifflinburg, 966-0341. Monday through Saturday.

Design Tiles, Mifflinburg, 966-3373. Monday through Friday or by appointment.

Penns Creek Pottery, Mifflinburg, 837-3809. Monday through Saturday.

Walnut Acres, Penns Creek, 800-433-3998. Store, Monday through Saturday; tours, Monday through Friday.

Millersburg Ferry, Millersburg, 692-2442. April through mid-November. Fee.

Centre County Lion Country Visitors & Convention Bureau, State College, 800-358-5466 or 814-231-1400.

Susquehanna Valley Visitors Bureau, Lewisburg (also Mifflinburg), 800-458-4748 or 524-7234.

8 ~

The Laurel Highlands

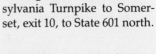

Getting there: Take the Pennsylvania Turnpike to Somerset, exit 10, to State 601 north.

Highlights: *A weekend's journey through the Laurel Highlands will thrill you with a whitewater rafting trip down the Youghigheny, pique your interest in the past by following historic thoroughfares such as the Forbes Road and the National Pike, and reveal sites as diverse as Frank Lloyd Wright's Fallingwater and Fort Necessity, where Col. George Washington lost a skirmish during the French and Indian War.*

The Route

From the Pennsylvania Turnpike Somerset exit 10, take State 601 north, State 985 north, and US 30 west to Laughlintown, Ligonier, and Greensburg. Pick up US 119 south in Greensburg, cross the turnpike at New Stanton, and continue south.

If you wish to shop at the Lenox Outlet or tour the Smith Glass Factory, take State 31 east near Mount Pleasant. Turn right at Factory or Poplar streets for the Glass Factory, or stay on State 31 for approximately 1 mile from town for Lenox.

Return to US 119 south to Uniontown, and connect with US 40 south to Farmington. Follow State 381 north through Ohiopyle to Normalville, and State 381/711 north to State 31/711 west to the Donegal exit (number 9) of the Pennsylvania Turnpike. The approximate total miles without side trips is 110.

The Laurel Highlands is a 100-mile region of mountains, forests of oak and hemlock, and hurrying streams. Scored by the massive Laurel and Chestnut ridges of the Alleghenies, it covers five counties of southwestern Pennsylvania. In winter, it is a skiers' playground at resorts such as Hidden Valley and Seven Springs; in spring, summer, and fall, its natural beauty and abundant outdoor recreational activities draw everyone from students on the trail of history to tanned kayakers whirling through the river rapids like multicolored tops.

Somerset is your port of entry into this rural Eden. North of town just beyond the junction of State 601 and State 985, the Somerset Historical Center tenders the story of western Pennsylvania's rural heritage. In this museum you're introduced to a way of life quite unlike that of the more civilized regions east of the Alleghenies.

The museum, which has outgrown its present buildings, is embarking on a multiyear expansion plan, which will not only change the physical layout but will place a much stronger emphasis on how industry helped the farmer and how the farmer reciprocated by providing necessary services to those working in industry.

Guided tours of the museum and grounds run about one and a half hours and encompass a maple sugar camp, where sugaring demonstrations are staged in late spring; the log barn; smokehouse; and Walter's Mill covered bridge. Both Hoffman and Fluck halls contain a variety of exhibits, such as an 1876 general store complete with potbelly stove and post office, an 1890 mail buggy, and a print shop with old presses and Linotypes. The present farmstead—the Adam Miller log house, circa 1850—will be moved to a new location, and the museum will also replicate dwellings representative of the pioneer period around 1790 and a more recent era, 1920.

At Jennerstown you join US 30, the Lincoln Highway, which in many sections follows historic Forbes Road, the 1758 route blazed by Col. Henry Bouquet and adopted by Gen. John Forbes in his march to capture Fort Duquesne during the French and Indian War.

At the foot of Laurel Mountain, the small village of Laughlintown and its more upscale neighbor, Ligonier, are well worth a day's investigation. The Ligonier Country Inn is a good base of operations. Its well-regarded restaurant specializes in American cuisine, and each of its twenty rooms is individually decorated with brass, canopy, or Shaker beds, Early American prints, and period furnishings.

Across the street, the Pie Shoppe Homestyle Bakery sends tantalizing aromas through the village from 7:00 A.M. to 6:00 P.M. daily. In addition to their sugary doughnuts and rich cakes and pies, they have a sandwich counter, handy for the makings of a midday picnic.

On a corner lot in the center of the borough, Robert Laughlin built the Compass Inn in 1799 as a stop for wayfarers on the Forbes Road. Passing through town in 1814 on his way to enter the Pittsburgh glass business, Robert Armor purchased the property, settled down, and became the proprietor of the prosperous hostelry. Five generations of the Armor family managed his holdings as an inn and, after 1862, as a private home.

Today the inn and its outbuildings are under the aegis of the Ligonier Historical Society, which maintains them as a museum. A costumed guide takes you through, pointing out details such as how, in the early days, stagecoaches and Conestoga wagons carrying herders and drovers, travelers, and salesmen paused for a hearty dinner of chicken and waffles and a drink of malt beer and brown sugar mulled with a hot poker. You'll see the military stove in the ladies' parlor, the men's dorms, which could sleep twenty-four in three double and three trundle beds, and a handsome old overland stage in the barn. Everything including the grounds has been expertly maintained, and the well-informed guides have many interesting tales to tell.

Just two miles from Laughlintown is Ligonier, whose picture-postcard square with its onion dome gazebo is the scene of summer band concerts from the end of May through August. Rimming the square (the local folks call it "The Diamond"), fine shops rub elbows with the sedate, white-columned town hall. The Ligonier Tavern on West Main is a popular watering hole specializing in Italian cuisine, and locals think well of the Colonial Inn on US 30 west of town.

Not just a shop stop, Ligonier has an interesting history dating back to the French and Indian War, when Gen. John Forbes fortified the location, naming it Fort Ligonier after Sir John Ligonier, commander in chief of Great Britain's military forces. Today you can tour twentieth-century Fort Ligonier, reconstructed on the site of the original 1758–1766 bastion using plans uncovered in a British library.

Your gateway to the complex is the spacious modern museum, where you will see *Post at Loyalhanna,* a film designed to introduce you to the era. Following the screening, you may stroll the north wing with its artifacts recovered from the site or tarry in the sumptuous period rooms, one inspired by Lord Ligonier's Georgian drawing room in London, the other the only room remaining from The Hermitage estate of soldier-statesman Arthur St. Clair.

Leaving the museum, you wander up the hill to the fort, which inside its palisade contains an officers' mess, soldiers' barracks, armory, hospital, commissary, officers' quarters, and the quartermaster's store. Buildings are "peopled" with full-size mannequin soldiers engaged in all sorts of activities, from card playing to aiding a doctor in a hospital operation. More realistic flesh and blood living history demonstrations take place through the season, and Fort Ligonier Days is celebrated each October.

The ride from Ligonier to Greensburg takes you through a beautiful rural landscape, with the Loyalhanna Creek bubbling along beside the road, sometimes to the right, sometimes dodging to the left. Area fishermen work the stream with graceful casts, their tiny insect imitations greedily snatched by hungry trout.

As you near the city, traffic and roadside congestion pick up. This seat of Westmoreland County is built on a hill, like so many southwestern Pennsylvania towns. The shining dome of the county courthouse is the most visible landmark, but your destination is the Westmoreland Museum of Art, which crowns the hill like some modern-day Acropolis.

The building and the funds to maintain it were a gift of Mary Marchand Woods, who bequeathed her entire estate for the construction and upkeep of the museum. Covering an entire city block, the Westmoreland would grace a metropolis larger than Greensburg. The permanent collection focuses on American art, with emphasis on nineteenth-century and southwestern Pennsylvania artists. Commonwealth painters such as Lancaster's Charles Demuth and the Brandywine's Andrew Wyeth are represented along with lesser known painters such as George Hetzel, Emil Bott, and Joseph Ryan Woodwell. Two sumptuous paneled rooms in the west wing feature a collection of eighteenth- and nineteenth-century American furniture, silver, Pittsburgh Bakewell glass, and paintings, including Rembrandt Peale's porthole "Portrait of George Washington."

While you're in Greensburg, you might want to detour a few miles north of the city on State 819, which connects with

SR 1032 east, to Historic Hanna's Town, the first county seat west of the Alleghenies. Costumed guides take you through the reconstructed courthouse/tavern, gaol, log palisade fort, and German Klingensmith House. The entire operation from docent service to building maintenance is staffed by volunteers from the Westmoreland County Historical Society.

From Hanna's Town go south through Greensburg, cross the Pennsylvania Turnpike, and head for Mount Pleasant and the L. E. Smith glass factory. Watch carefully for the small sign designating your turn.

The process of making glassware by hand is the oldest industry in America and one that is fascinating to watch. "Gatherers" withdraw the molten glass from the furnace with a "punty," or iron rod, and transfer it to a mold. The piece is cooled, then hand finished and polished. At tour's end, you have the opportunity to visit the outlet, where you can purchase pieces from the regular line as well as irregulars at 20 to 70 percent off retail.

A mile east of town, Lenox, manufacturers of fine china and crystal, have two retail facilities in addition to their massive stemware plant. The Lenox Shop carries the company's full line from wineglasses to place settings; the Warehouse handles both second-quality and first-quality discontinued merchandise. The Shop exacts full retail, but the Warehouse reduces second-quality stock by 35 to 50 percent and discontinued items by 50 to 75 percent.

After rejoining US 119, you head south to Uniontown, where you join US 40, the route of the National Pike, the nation's first transportation link from the East to the western frontier. It's a long pull over Summit Mountain, but after an equally daunting downhill run you pass through the small community of Chalk Hill and come to Fort Necessity National Battlefield. Visitors have the opportunity to tour the bastion, explore wooded walking trails, and inspect the Mount Washington Tavern, built about 1827 to service travelers on the National Road.

Anyone who arrives expecting something on the magnitude of Valley Forge or Gettysburg will be disappointed. Fort Necessity is small and compact—a product of the French and Indian Wars. The reconstructed stockade, storehouse, and entrenchments reflect both the era and the condition of the fort's design.

Constructed in 1754 at Great Meadows, as the site was then known, Fort Necessity was Col. George Washington's attempt to fortify the strategic area following the French defeat at Jumonville. On July 3, 1754, the French attacked the small outpost with 600 of their troops and 100 Indians, and although the colonials were defeated, Washington was allowed to withdraw with honors of war, retaining arms and baggage.

Just beyond the battlefield, State 381 heads north to Ohiopyle. On a sunny spring day the state park at the base of the falls is dotted with rubber rafts carrying adventurers in all manner of dress, from full wet suits to shorts. These white-water enthusiasts are preparing to enter the lower Youghigheny's six major rapids, which will propel them 7.5 miles downstream to Bruner Run.

Four professional outfitters provide guided raft trips on the "Yough" (say Yok), and their safety record is good. They fit each rafter with a class 5 life jacket, and an experienced river guide gives a thorough briefing on what to expect and how to handle both body and boat.

Those more content to stay on dry land will find an abundance of hiking trails in the state park. Ferncliff Peninsula, formed by a great natural bend in the river, has been designated a Natural Landmark, and its trails are popular favorites. There are bike rentals in town, and a ten-mile bike trail runs along an abandoned railroad right-of-way connecting

Rafting the Youghigheny

Ohiopyle with Confluence. Site of the Youghigheny Dam with its popular boating lake, Confluence is also home to River's Edge Cafe, a restaurant famous for its pastas, fresh salads and seafood, and chargrilled chicken. On a sunny afternoon the cafe porch is packed with famished bikers and those who come from Ohiopyle by car over Sugarloaf Mountain.

Just north of Ohiopyle, one of America's true architectural gems serenely spans a woodland stream in the depth of a mossy glen. Fallingwater was designed in 1936 by Frank Lloyd Wright as a vacation retreat for Pittsburgh department store magnate Edgar J. Kaufmann. Called "the most famous private residence ever built," it is one of the finest examples of its creator's concept of organic architecture—a building shaped by and conforming to its site.

The multilevel house with its strong horizontal lines was erected over a waterfall on Bear Run, a free-flowing mountain stream. Constructed of native sandstone, with stone piers separating reinforced concrete cantilevers, the building is one with the water, rocks, and forest.

Visiting Fallingwater should be an ongoing endeavor, because each trip reveals another delightful aspect of Wright's genius: the master bedroom with corner casement windows, which open to reveal no intersection support to block the view; or the living room hatchway, which permits access to the brook and provides cooling breezes in summer.

Tours take approximately forty-five minutes, although it is easy to spend two to three hours total on the tour proper, perusing the exhibits at the handsome visitors center, browsing in the bookstore's excellent selection of architectural tomes and attractive gifts, walking the nature trail, and visiting the cafe for some light refreshment. The walk to the house may be a bit challenging for the unsure of foot; accommodations for the disabled are available by making prior arrangements.

One of the most popular attractions of the Laurel Highlands, Fallingwater hosts more than 130,000 visitors a year, and spring and summer weekends are extremely busy. It is very important to avoid disappointment by calling ahead to reserve your tour time. Try to go during the week, if possible.

For those wishing to stay overnight before returning to the turnpike, Mountain Trees between Farmington and Flatrock, or Glades Pike Inn on State 31 between Donegal and Somerset, are good choices. Mountain Trees is a large converted doctor's residence with pleasant, sunny rooms and an ebullient proprietor. Helen Helpy's breakfasts leave you staggering from the table, and she is happy to share her legendary corn bread recipe with all who ask.

Glades Pike Inn is a handsome 1842 brick residence that once served as a stagecoach stop. Popular with winter skiers and summer wanderers, the bed and breakfast retains its nineteenth-century charm while allowing its guests the luxury of twentieth-century improvements, such as private baths.

In the Area

All numbers are within area code 412 unless otherwise indicated.

Somerset Historical Center, Somerset, 814-445-6077. Closed Mondays. Fee.

Ligonier Country Inn, Laughlintown, 238-3651.

The Pie Shoppe Homestyle Bakery, Laughlintown, 238-9628.

The Compass Inn Museum, Laughlintown, 238-4983. May through the last weekend in October. Closed Monday. Fee.

The Ligonier Tavern, Ligonier, 238-4831.

The Colonial Inn, Ligonier, 238-6604.

Fort Ligonier, Ligonier, 238-9701. April 1 through October 31. Fee.

Westmoreland Museum of Art, Greensburg, 837-1500. Closed Monday.

Historic Hanna's Town, Greensburg, 836-1800. Fee.

Smith Glass Outlet and Factory Tour, Mount Pleasant, 547-3544. Outlet, Monday through Friday and holidays from January through March 31. Tours, Monday through Friday except the first two weeks of July and the last week of December.

The Lenox Shop and Warehouse Outlet, Mount Pleasant, 547-9555.

Fort Necessity National Battlefield, Farmington, 329-5512. Fee.

Guided whitewater rafting on the Youghigheny. Spring through fall. Reservations required. Fee.

Wilderness Voyageurs, Ohiopyle, 800-272-4141.

White Water Adventurers, Ohiopyle, 800-WWA- RAFT.

Laurel Highlands River Tours, Ohiopyle, 800-472-3846.3846

Mountain Streams, Ohiopyle, 800-245-4090.

Ohiopyle State Park, Ohiopyle, 329-8591.

River's Edge Cafe and Bed and Breakfast, Confluence, 814-395-5059. Cafe, Friday through Sunday, April and May, and Labor Day weekend through October 31; Tuesday through Sunday from Memorial Day weekend through Labor Day.

Fallingwater, Mill Run, 329-8501. Closed Monday from April through mid-November; weekends, weather permitting, from Mid-November through March. Reservations recommended. Fee.

Mountain Trees, Markleysburg, 329-1020.

Glades Pike Inn, Somerset, 814-443-4978.

Laurel Highlands, Ligonier, 800-925-7669 or 238-5661.

9 ~

North Central Rambles

Getting there: From Williamsport take US 220 west.

Highlights: *For a long weekend's journey into the north woods, stay cozy in a buffalo plaid jacket from Woolrich, drive the wilds west of Pine Creek Gorge and see deer or wild turkey, visit Pennsylvania's Grand Canyon, stroll the gaslit streets of Wellsboro, and discover a lumberman's life.*

The Route

From Williamsport, take US 220 west to the Woolrich/McElhatten exit. At the stop sign, turn right and go 3.5 miles through McElhatten to Woolrich. Leaving the Woolrich store, turn left, bear right past the mill and left at the Y onto Dutch Hollow Road, which connects with State 44. Follow State 44 west and State 414 west toward Blackwell. If the weather has been dry, you can pick up the West Rim dirt road by taking a left just south of Blackwell. After six miles, make a sharp right on the Painter/Leetonia Road for two miles, another right for two miles on Thompson Hollow Road, and finally a right onto Colton Road, which brings you out near Colton State Park and Ansonia. Turn east on US 6 to Wellsboro. In bad weather, stay on State 414 to State 287 north into Wellsboro.

In Wellsboro, take State 660 west to Leonard Harrison State Park and State 362 to the link with US 6 west. In Sweden Valley, turn east on State 44, which becomes State 44/144 in the five miles from Carter Camp to Oleona. In Oleona, State 44 resumes. Continue south to State 973 east and Salladasburg, where you pick up State 287 south to Jersey Shore and US 220. The approximate total miles is 202.

Contrary to popular belief, it's Pennsylvania, not Maine, that is home to Woolrich, the well-known manufacturer of outdoor wear. In 1830 John Rich founded his company in this tiny north central town. The operation began as a mill to sell yarns, cover-lids, blankets, flannel cloth, and socks to lumbermen. Before the turn of the century, it began manufacturing the woolen garments for which it has become famous, and in recent years the corporation has diversified into other types of sportswear.

Ever since 1845 Woolrich has had a company store, although it has grown from a simple room at the mill to its present size, complete with Village Cafe and bank autoteller machine. There are racks and racks of men's and women's clothing, some youth's wear, the classic department for sportsmen, a fabric center where woolens are sold by the pound, the "Backroom" for irregulars and seconds, and the "Cover Up" shop, where you can purchase fine woolen blankets and European down comforters. The Boy Scout motto is "be prepared," and if you choose to begin your journey in Woolrich, you will be well suited to any contingency the north woods can offer.

From Woolrich, Dutch Hollow Road follows a feeder stream of Pine Creek until it debouches into the main flow at the junction of State 44. The next miles twist and turn through Tiadaghton State Forest, following the bends in the river. At Slate Run, Tom and Debbie Finkbinder run Wolfe's General Store and Slate Run Tackle Shop, where you can stop for groceries, souvenirs, last-minute supplies, or a fishing license. Pine Creek draws many trout fishermen, and as an authorized Orvis dealer Tom caters to the trade with more than 300 types of trout flies, a wide selection of rods and reels, fishing vests, waders, and the like.

A few miles farther down the road, the Cedar Run Inn offers comfortable lodging and well-prepared meals for hikers, bikers, canoeists, fishermen, or folks just wanting to get away from it all. Stan and Charlotte Dudkin make everyone feel welcome, whether you're a couch potato or a fitness enthusiast, and there's always genial conversation around morning coffee in the sitting room.

If you enjoy hiking, one of the state's finest day treks is easily accessed from the inn. The Golden Eagle, a nine-mile trail with a vertical rise of 2,100 feet, takes approximately six to seven hours and passes through meadows filled with wildflowers, stands of mature trees, thickets of mountain laurel, and evidence of early lumbering activity. The trailhead is a little more than five miles south of the inn on State 414. Marked with an orange blaze, the path begins on the far side of the railroad tracks and makes a loop through portions of Wolf Run Wild Area and State Game Lands. The Dudkins can show you many alternatives, either more or less challenging, and they stock a large supply of area trail maps and books delineating excursions.

Leaving Cedar Run, it's about five miles to Blackwell and the turnoff for the dirt road that takes you up the West Rim of Pine Creek Gorge. If the weather has been dry, the route is fine for any touring car, but if there has been a lot of rain, the alternative of taking State 287 in Morris is advisable.

The West Rim Road leads through some pretty wild country in Tioga State Forest, and every now and then an intriguing vista opens up. If you pass at the right time of day, you
might see white-tailed deer, ruffed grouse, wild turkey, even
black bear. You eventually emerge at Colton Point State Park,
one of the twin parks that frame what is dubbed Pennsylvania's Grand Canyon. Now, anyone who has seen both the
Arizona and Pennsylvania versions will attest that they
haven't a whole lot in common, except that they are both
gorges and both contain a river. That notwithstanding, Pine
Creek Gorge is beautiful in its own way—fifty miles long and
1,000 feet deep, its rocky walls tree-lined, waterfalls lacing
down its sides, and a sliver of glistening water winding
through the heart of the canyon.

Those of strong legs and ample wind can descend to the
canyon floor by way of the popular Turkey Path. It's 2.5 miles
of up-and-down switchbacks; the trailhead is just before the
paved cul-de-sac at the park.

A less taxing alternative is the two-mile Barbour Rock–
West Rim Loop, which traces the canyon rim and provides
magnificent panoramas. The blue-blazed trail leaves the parking area on the east side of Colton Road, intersects with the
orange-blazed West Rim Trail, leads south along the gorge
rim, and finally rejoins Colton Road.

When you arrive in Wellsboro, you are immediately
impressed with its similarity to a New England town. The
wide main street with its old-fashioned gas street lamps and
the village green with its commemorative statues and facing
of churches looks like a Connecticut transplant. Although
founded in 1806 by settlers from Delaware, Maryland, and
Philadelphia, this Tioga county seat was part of the Connecticut Grant, and many of the residents were from the north.
They built large, gracious homes with spacious yards and
planted stately elms and maples along the avenues.

The Tioga County courthouse in Wellsboro

Today Wellsboro is a quiet, hospitable town, and most of the year people just go about their business without a lot of fuss. The two exceptions to this trend are during the foliage season, when it seems as if the whole world has discovered this charming village, and during the annual Laurel Festival, the third weekend in June, when everyone turns out for a big parade, a carnival, and the crowning of a state laurel queen from candidates representing north central Pennsylvania high schools.

If you're in town on a more sedate weekend, drive out to Leonard Harrison State Park for a view of the other side of the canyon, or look up Chuck Dillon at Pine Creek Outfitters near the US 6 entrance to Colton State Park. Chuck is the twentieth-century equivalent of Nessmuck, Wellsboro's nature writer of the nineteenth century, and he is the guru of the north central adventure excursions, whether your taste runs to a float trip on Pine Creek or a hike in the woods.

If you stay in town, stroll down past the courthouse to the green, wander the paths shaded by arching trees, and visit the fountain with the statue of Wynken, Blynken, and Nod in their wooden shoe. Check out the local gossip at the Wellsboro Diner on the corner of Main Street and East Avenue. This wonderful relic hasn't changed much since its installation in 1939, and its daily specials still include crowd pleasers such as meat loaf and mashed potatoes and gravy, topped off with a slice of lemon meringue pie for dessert.

If you hanker for a more genteel atmosphere, the Penn Wells Hotel has an attractive dining room serving daily specials from Sunday's brunch to Thursday's roast prime rib of beef. Don't neglect to inspect the unusual American flag displayed in the lobby. Made entirely of 1,438 red, white, and blue Christmas tree ornaments manufactured at the Wellsboro plant of the Corning Glass Works, the six-foot, ten-inch by ten-foot, eight-inch flag graced the cover of *Life* magazine in 1950.

One of the town's nicest bed and breakfasts is Debbie and Charles Keister's Four Winds on West Avenue. Built in the early 1870s for the Landrus family, the Victorian "painted lady" has gray siding with mauve, rose, and Navajo pink trim. The floor-to-ceiling windows admit generous amounts of light, and Debbie's deft touch with antiques dispels the notion that all Victorian decor is dour and dark.

Leaving Wellsboro, head toward Galeton and the Pennsylvania Lumber Museum. If you're the slightest bit hungry, stop at the Ansonia Gulf Station, where they serve monster ice-cream cones from Sunset ice cream made in Williamsport. Their small cone equals a large double in most places.

The Lumber Museum is located halfway between Galeton and Sweden Valley, across from Denton Hill Ski Area. With more than 3,000 artifacts and objects, the museum displays interpret Pennsylvania's lumbering heritage of the last century, when white pine and hemlock were the green gold of the area. Not utilizing mere static displays, the museum has constructed a logging camp of the era, complete with bunkhouse and mess hall, blacksmith and carpenter's shops, stable and hay barn for the horses, and a functioning sawmill. An engine house shelters Shay locomotive CN-2598 from the Lima, Ohio, works. Last used in the mid-1950s, it is the "stemwinder" variety and was the most popular of the geared locomotives because of its good traction on steep grades and sharp curves.

Every year on the Fourth of July weekend, the museum sponsors the Bark Peelers' Convention, a two-day celebration of woodsmen's skills. There's log burling on the millpond and demonstrations of sawing, chopping, hewing, blacksmithing, bark peeling, and down-home fiddling. The steam-powered circular sawmill is in operation, and there are special events and a craft show.

From Sweden Valley to Haneyville, it's pretty much a straight shot through Susquehannock and Sproul State forests until you reach the turnoff for State 293 and Salladasburg. What distinguishes this small village from other whistle-stops along the way is Cohick's Trading Post. Founded in 1924 by J.J. Cohick and still run by his son Bob, the store is a U.S. post office and general emporium extraordinary, where you can buy everything from a can of beans to a hunting rifle. There's hardware, hunting and fishing gear and licenses, groceries, shoes, a small drugstore, videos, pots and pan, souvenirs, cold cuts, and scrapple—all watched over by the glass-eyed stare of mounted moose, deer, and caribou.

The luncheonette lists six varieties of homemade soup and twelve flavors of ice cream, including teaberry and chocolate malt. Daily specials run to items such as a hot roast beef sandwich with fries and fresh fruit cocktail for $2.50. On the fifth counter stool from the right, there's a sign, "Red Grange sat here."

Before finishing your journey at Jersey Shore, pause a while in Salladasburg, population 250. Buy an ice-cream cone, share a bench with a friend, enjoy the sun, and, if for just a short while, become part of a gentler time.

In the Area

All numbers are within area code 717 unless otherwise indicated.

The Woolrich Store, Woolrich, 769-7401. Closed Sunday and holidays.

Wolfe's General Store and Slate Run Tackle Shop, Slate Run, 753-8551.

Cedar Run Inn, Cedar Run, 353-6241. Restaurant closed for dinner Monday and Tuesday and every Sunday except during October.

Department of Environmental Resources, Bureau of Forestry, Harrisburg, 783-7941 (state forest maps).

Leonard Harrison and Colton Point state parks, Wellsboro, 724-3061.

Pine Creek Outfitters, Wellsboro, 724-3003.

Wellsboro Diner, Wellsboro, 724-3992.

Penn Wells Hotel, Wellsboro, 724-2111.

Four Winds Bed & Breakfast, Wellsboro, 800-368-7963 or 724-6141.

Ansonia Gulf Station, Ansonia, 724-4034.

Pennsylvania Lumber Museum, Galeton, 814-435-2652.

Cohick's Trading Post, Salladasburg, 398-0311.

Tioga Association for Recreation and Tourism (Wellsboro), 800-332-6718 in PA, 724-1926 out-of-state.

Lycoming County Tourist Promotion Agency, Williamsport (Salladasburg and Cedar Run), 800-358-9900 or 321-1200.

10 ~

Allegheny Ridge

Getting there: Take the Pennsylvania Turnpike to Bedford, exit 11, to US 220 north.

Highlights: *For a two- or three-day excursion into the history of man's attempts to tame the Allegheny Ridge, visit Altoona with its Horseshoe Curve and Railroad Museum, or relive the horror of the great Johnstown Flood at the site of the failed dam in Saint Michael and in the city itself at the Johnstown Flood Museum. Hunt the flotsam and jetsam of the past at the profusion of antique shops in the old canal town of Hollidaysburg and in neighboring Duncansville.*

The Route

Leave the Pennsylvania Turnpike at Bedford, exit 11, and take US 220 north to Altoona. Follow signs to the Railroaders Memorial Museum. US 220 south connects to US 22 west for Duncansville and east to Hollidaysburg.

To visit the Horseshoe Curve, return to Altoona, and take Broad Avenue to 40th Street, which connects to SR 4008. Leaving the Curve for the Allegheny Portage Railroad, follow the "trailblazer" directional road signs of the Southwestern Pennsylvania Heritage Route Guide by taking SR 1034 west, SR 1015 south, SR 2016 west, and US 22 west.

To reach Saint Michael, continue west on US 22 to US 219 south. Turn on State 869 for the Johnstown Flood National Memorial. Rejoin US 219 south to the intersection of State 56 west to Johnstown.

Leaving Johnstown, take US 219 south to State 281 south, which connects with the Somerset entrance (number 10) to the Pennsylvania Turnpike. The approximate total miles is 109.

As you leave the Pennsylvania Turnpike at Bedford and drive north toward Altoona, try to imagine the time when the Allegheny Ridge presented an almost insurmountable obstacle to America's westward expansion. It poses little difficulty to modern transportation, but rising steeply 1,200 feet above Altoona and Hollidaysburg, it offered a challenge to nineteenth-century planners and builders determined to forge a passage through the barrier.

Altoona sits at the base of the ridge, its long, narrow layout determined by the great Pennsylvania Railroad's Juniata rail yards, portions of which are still in use by Conrail as a primary locomotive repair and maintenance facility. Today the Railroaders Memorial Museum collection of rolling stock and railroad memorabilia captures the quality of the railroad known worldwide as "The Standard" for its fastidious testing of all phases of operation. Pictures and exhibits delineate how locomotives were run on treadmills to determine wear and tear, and how bushels of oranges were squeezed to find the juiciest, best-tasting variety for the dining cars.

Young rail fans will enjoy the immense working model train exhibit. Those with a reverence for the past will appreciate Memorial Hall, its walls emblazoned with the names of the railroad workers, from the Irish who built the Horseshoe Curve to shop workers of today.

In the yard, a collection of rolling stock includes the state's official steam locomotive, the K-4, #1361, built right here in the Altoona yards; steam and diesel locomotives; dining and sleeper cars; a post office car; and the Loretto, the elegant private railcar of steel magnate Charles Schwab.

Visitors to the Ninth Avenue site will find a busy construction area in the next few years. As part of one of Pennsylvania's new heritage parks, the museum is being moved from its current cramped quarters to its permanent location in the former Pennsylvania Railroad Master Mechanics Building. This will not happen overnight, and although construction may at times limit access to certain exhibits, the final result should more than compensate for temporary inconvenience.

Before leaving the city, you might visit Baker Mansion and the nearby Allegheny iron furnace to get a glimpse of Altoona's history before the coming of the railroad. Currently the home of the Blair County Historical Society, the mansion has twenty-eight rooms housing a collection of period furnishings and artifacts.

South of Altoona, the quiet streets of Hollidaysburg and Duncansville play host to antique hunters who travel long distances to visit the many shops that line US Business Route 22. Dealers in this area once marketed wholesale only, but over the years many have opened retail shops, which in turn have attracted still more retailers to the region.

In Hollidaysburg, Tom Burkholder is one of these veteran wholesalers with a retail store, The Antique Outlet, which stocks some furniture and a large selection of glass, china, and kitchen items. On Allegheny Street, Faye Weaver's elegant Remember When is a multidealer, general-line shop. Built by partner Joe Pasi from the ground up for the specific purpose of displaying antiques, it has the distinction of being one of the most attractive shops you'll find anywhere.

In Duncansville, David Donnelly's shops flank the road, one dealing in thirty years' accumulation of everything from Victorian furniture to toys, and the other specializing in architectural antiques. On Third Avenue, Cathy Jo Wertz presides over her Creekside Antiques Co-op with the tolerant benevolence of a den mother. At Dodson's Antiques, Marian Dodson brings fifty-two years of experience to her shop, which features a dazzling display of American cut crystal, art glass, and sterling, plus a general line. Other traders too numerous to detail make the twin towns a "must" stop for antique mavens.

If all this shopping gives you an appetite, head for The Dream in Hollidaysburg. Originally a diner and now a family restaurant cum bakery, The Dream serves sandwiches on homemade breads, and daily specials ranging from Tuesday's roast turkey and waffles to Saturday's country-style ribs. Save room for yummy desserts such as apple dumplings or Boston cream pie.

Well fortified and ready to take on the mountains, head back to Altoona and follow the well-marked Heritage Trail signs to the Horseshoe Curve, a National Historic Landmark. The history of the Curve is tied inexorably to man's effort to tame the Alleghenies and allow westward expansion of people and materials. For a time this was achieved through the Allegheny Portage Railroad, a system that allowed the Pennsylvania Mainline Canal to traverse the Alleghenies by means of a series of inclined planes connected by track.

The birth of the Pennsylvania Railroad in the 1840s made an all-rail route necessary, and engineers were faced with the problem of setting track over 2,300-foot-high Allegheny Mountain. The mountain was too steep for conventional construction, so engineer and company president J. Edgar Thompson devised the ingenious solution of a doubling-back loop to gradually scale the summit. The proof of his genius lies in the fact that from the day it opened in 1854, the Curve has served the railroads with the major passageway over the Alleghenies. Constructed entirely by hand with pick and shovel, it still meets the needs of today's railroad industry.

When you visit the site, you will find a tidy visitors center patterned after the old Kittanning Point railroad station. Interpretive exhibits tell the story of the Curve's construction, and there is a well-done seven-minute film introduction to the history of transportation in general and the Curve in particular. From the visitors center, you may ride the funicular to trackside, or if you feel extraordinarily ambitious, a flight of 194 steps will take you puffing to the summit. Trains run every fifteen minutes or so, and it is a glorious sight to see the long Conrail freights completely outline the Curve.

When you depart, you will be following country lanes back in time to the era preceding that of the shaping of the Curve. The Allegheny Portage Railroad National Historic Site was constructed between 1831 and 1834. Not a part of the nation's rail network, rather it was a means of traversing the Alleghenies and bridging east and west waterways through a series of inclined planes connected by sections of track.

Leaving the Pennsylvania Mainline Canal basin at Hollidaysburg, the packet boat sections from Philadelphia were floated onto railroad cars for the portage. Hauled from the water by stationary steam engines, they were then pulled by locomotives over the long grade to the base of the first incline, where workers hitched three cars at a time to the continuous cable moving over the rails. Powered by another stationary engine, the cars were then transported over five inclines up and five inclines down the mountain. On the grades between planes, the cars were drawn by horses or locomotives. The boats were again launched into the water at the Johnstown canal basin and continued their journey to Pittsburgh.

At the site off US 22 east of Cresson, you will find more work in progress. The attractive native stone visitors center offers displays and a twenty-minute film relating to the Portage Railroad. From the center, an eighth-mile boardwalk leads through the woods to an old stone quarry and finally to the top of Incline No. 6, the summit level, where the National

Park Service has constructed a representation of Engine House No. 6. Plans for the future include reestablishment of a section of track and restoration of the Lemon House, Samuel Lemon's hotel and tavern, which once accommodated the hundreds of canal and railroad passengers crossing the mountains.

If you are to understand the tragedy at Johnstown on May 31, 1889, you must stop first at Saint Michael and see what remains of the dam that failed and sent a thirty-five-foot-high wall of water down the valley of the Little Conemaugh, killing more than 2,000 and laying waste what had been a prosperous steel city. From the heights of the National Park Service visitors center, you can still discern the outlines of the lake, now a grassy depression, and the worn abutments of the dam through which a docile creek now flows. Through the trees you can see the roofs of the village of Saint Michael, which grew around the cottages and clubhouse of the South Fork Fishing and Hunting Club, once the summer retreat of wealthy Pittsburghers such as Andrew Carnegie and Henry Clay Frick.

Go inside the center and see the film *Black Friday*, but be warned—it is the stuff of nightmares. The film is so powerful and its portrayal so graphic that it might not be appropriate for some children; a parental caveat is posted on the auditorium doors.

The story of the great flood is the tale of nature's revenge at man's carelessness. Johnstown in 1889 was a steel company town of German and Welsh, its population of 30,000 crowded on the floodplain where Stony Creek and the Little Conemaugh meet. Problems with yearly flooding had increased as hillsides were denuded for wood and streambeds were narrowed with fill for additional building land.

The people of Johnstown were used to the seasonal overflows caused by heavy rains, and they had come to accept

another potential threat—the South Fork Dam, which held
two-mile-long Lake Conemaugh in check fourteen miles from
the city. The dam once held auxiliary water for the Mainline
Canal system, but when that went under and was purchased
by the Pennsylvania Railroad, the earthen works fell into disrepair. In 1862 a break occurred near the discharge pipes, but
there was little damage because of low water levels. The railroad abandoned the dam, the discharge pipes were sold as
scrap, and the dam deteriorated until it was purchased by the
South Fork Club.

The citizens of Johnstown were certain that such a
wealthy and illustrious group of industrialists would maintain
the seventy-two-foot-high dam. They would have been more
wary had they seen the shoddy repairs, the fish trap above
the spillway that collected debris, the two- to four-foot sag in
the dam's center, and the lowering of the dam face to accom-
modate the members' carriages. Discharge pipes were never
replaced, making slow release of water impossible in times of
deluge.

By the time the record rains fell the night of May 31, the
elements were all in place for tragedy. Spring precipitation
had been above average, and Johnstown was already awash
in two to seven feet of water. At 4:07 P.M., people heard "a
roar like thunder," and twenty million tons of water broke
from the ruined dam and swept down the valley in a lethal
wave, carrying freight cars and locomotives, sections of track,
houses and trees, men and animals, living and dead, toward
the stone railroad bridge, where the debris piled up in a forty-
five-acre mass against the arches. A violent wind preceded
the horror, and survivors remember the accompanying black
pall of smoke and steam, the "death mist," created by the
explosion of boilers in the mills.

Some reached the safety of the hillsides, and some rode
the wreckage down the Conemaugh, praying for rescue. Oth-
ers trapped in miles of barbed wire were included in the

deadly brew when the wire works was destroyed. Adding to the carnage was the fire in the oil-soaked debris at the bridge. Many perished while rescuers tried in vain to free them.

When it was all over, 2,209 died in the flood and 40 more in the typhoid epidemic that followed. Some of the bodies were never identified but were buried in the "Unknown Plot" in the city's Grandview Cemetery. Property damage was $17 million and cleanup took years; although the city rebuilt its manufacturing centers, it never reached the industrial prominence it had before man forced nature's hand in the worst flood disaster in the nation's history.

When you visit the city, you will see little evidence of scars. A few of the old pre-flood buildings still stand, such as the Franklin Street United Methodist Church and Alma Hall, which sheltered 300 survivors that terrible night.

The yellow brick Carnegie library has been transformed into the Johnstown Flood Museum, where visitors can watch Charles Guggenheim's Academy Award-winning documentary and scrutinize top-flight exhibits depicting the story through photos, videos, and artifacts. A simulation of bridge rubble lines the back wall, with bits of trees, houses, locomotives, and rail. A case contains poignant bits of authentic flood-washed memorabilia: a child's shoe, a calico dress, a carpenter's box. A bottle of flood water, black and greasy, stands on a pedestal. A diorama traces the actual course of flood waters down the valley.

As an antidote to the catastrophe, the museum focuses not just on the melancholy aftereffects of the disaster, but it also celebrates the resilience of the human spirit by illustrating how the people of the city fought back, rebuilt their homes and businesses, and got on with their lives.

Johnstown today is a clean city of ethnic neighborhoods. No sooty smoke belches from steel mill stacks, and Central Park is abloom with flowers. Every fifteen minutes the Incline

climbs the precipitous slopes of Westmont Hill to give home-
owners access to suburban heights and provide visitors with
an unexcelled view of the city and the Conemaugh Valley.

From the observation deck and the hilltop restaurant you
can see Cambria City, the town's best-known blue-collar
neighborhood. On Labor Day weekend the area hosts the
annual FolkFest, with food booths lining Chestnut Street and
music filling the air. The enticing aromas are said to carry all
the way downtown. Area churches such as the German
Immaculate Conception and Slovak Saint Stephens open their
doors to visitors, and a variety of performing arts are presented on three stages.

If you want a real Johnstown experience but can't make
the festival, stop at the Phoenix Tavern in Cambria City for
lunch or dinner. The place is a no-nonsense neighborhood
eatery and watering hole, and although there are daily specials, the traditional *pirohi* (ravioli-style noodles stuffed with
cheese-flavored mashed potatoes) and *huluska* (cabbage and
noodles) are served every Friday. If you want a seat, you'd
better be through the tavern door as early as possible, since
locals flock to the spot.

Johnstown is not long on quaint country inns, but just
outside of town Andy Fedore and MaryLou Astorino have
enlarged and transformed an old one-room schoolhouse into
a beautiful and gracious bed and breakfast. MaryLou gives
Andy credit for the artistic inspiration, which makes Meadowbrook attractive, with its country decor, stenciled walls,
old quilts, and antiques. MaryLou is coexecutor of Andy's
ideas as well as cook extraordinaire. Oh, those raspberry
orange muffins and egg frittata filled with fresh veggies!

In the Area

All numbers are within area code 814 unless otherwise noted.

Altoona Railroaders Memorial Museum and The Horseshoe
Curve National Historic Landmark, Altoona, 946-0834.
Museum and Curve, daily from May through October;
closed Monday from November through April. Curve
funicular closed for maintenance first Tuesday of the
month in summer. Fee for funicular.

Baker Mansion, Altoona, 942-3916. Tuesday through
Saturday from Memorial Day through Labor Day;
weekends only from mid-April through May and
September through October. Fee.

The Antique Outlet, Hollidaysburg, 695-4848. Closed
Sunday and Monday.

Remember When, Hollidaysburg, 695-2667.

David Donnelly Antiques, Duncansville, 695-5942. Closed
Sunday.

Donnelly's Outdoors, Duncansville, 695-5508. Closed
Sunday.

Creekside Antiques Co-op, Duncansville, 695-5520.

Dodson's Antiques, Duncansville, 695-1901. Closed Sunday.

The Dream, Hollidaysburg, 696-3384.

Allegheny Portage Railroad National Historic Site, Cresson,
886-6150.

Johnstown Flood National Memorial, Saint Michael,
495-4643.

The Johnstown Flood Museum, Johnstown, 539-1889. Fee.

Johnstown Inclined Plane, Johnstown, 536-1816.

Phoenix Tavern, Johnstown, 536-3981. Closed Sunday.

Meadowbrook School Bed & Breakfast, Johnstown, 539-1756.

Convention and Visitors Bureau of Blair County, Altoona
(Altoona, Hollidaysburg, and Duncansville),
800-842-5866 or 943-4183 (Southwestern Pennsylvania
Heritage Route Guide).

Cambria County Tourist Council, Johnstown (Johnstown
FolkFest), 800-237-8590 (PA, OH, MD) or 536-7993.

11 ~

Old Communities of the Southwest

Getting there: Leave I-80 at exit 1 to State 60 south and State 208 east.

Highlights: *Your weekend visit to the southwest begins in beautiful New Wilmington with its graceful homes, maple tree–lined streets, and large population of Yellow Buggy Amish. From here you travel to Volant with its antiques; Grove City, site of August Wendell Forge; Slippery Rock with its college and environmental center; Lake Arthur with Moraine and McConnells Mill state parks; and finally to Harmony and Old Economy, homes of one of America's most successful early Christian communal societies.*

The Route

Crossing the Pennsylvania/Ohio border on I-80, leave the highway at exit 1 and take State 60 south and State 208 east through New Wilmington and Volant. In Grove City follow State 173 south to Slippery Rock and Stone House. Turn south on State 528 and west on US 422, which skirts Lake Arthur's western shore. Near McConnells Mill, take US 19 south, which routes you to Zelienople, where you catch State 68 west and State 989 south to Ambridge. In Ambridge follow State 65 south for seven miles, which leads to I-79 just north of Pittsburgh. The approximate total miles is seventy-seven.

If the state of Pennsylvania held a contest for its prettiest small town, New Wilmington would rank among the top five finishers. The peaceful borough is everyone's "Our Town," with Westminster College campus, stately, thriving downtown, and graceful old buildings, such as the Tavern Inn, part of the underground railroad during the Civil War.

New Wilmington is surrounded by farmland, much of it expertly tilled by Old Order Amish. Their tidy farms are a monument to husbandry, and their quiet presence in town lends a special dimension to village life. Smart horse-drawn buggies rattle through town on errands; it is not at all unusual to see an Amish mother with her well-behaved children head down Market Street to the Quilting Bee for sewing supplies. Every year on the third Saturday of April and October, the local Grange Hall sponsors a quilt auction, which rivals Harrisburg's Mennonite Relief Sale in size. More than 350 quilts ranging in size from wall hangings to full size are auctioned off.

These Plain People belong to one of the most conservative Amish groups, and here, away from the mainstream tourist trade, they are allowed to come and go in peace. It is a tribute to the townspeople that they treat them as neighbors, not as a commodity to be exploited. Camera-toting tourists are politely requested to respect the Amish regard for privacy and keep their photographic efforts confined to the scenery or the "English," as the Amish call those not of their faith.

Downtown has an active commercial center, with a wide assortment of shops and restaurants ranging from Isaly's, with its skyscraper ice-cream cones, to the elegant Tavern, where the excellence of cuisine is matched by the attentive service. At lunch, you'll be in hot competition with local residents for a seat at the Feed Mill Tea Room on the corner of Vine and Market.

Behm's Bed and Breakfast on Waugh Avenue is just a block away from the Westminster College quad. Bob and Nancy Behm's cheerful 1895 home boasts immaculate, well-appointed rooms and a wide porch with wicker rockers—just the place to wile away a summer afternoon. Nancy is a talented watercolor artist, and a collection of her works is displayed in her studio and throughout the house.

Shoppers can browse in a variety of gift shops, including some specializing in Amish-made crafts, or take a short ride out of town to the Apple Castle for fresh cider and crisp apples. Antique lovers will especially enjoy Patrick Henry Antiques & Collectibles right on South Market. The sunny, brick, nineteenth-century residence-turned-shop is chockablock with everything from handsome gateleg tables to Victorian tussie-mussies.

Just down State 208 at a bend in the road, the borough of Volant has been transmogrified from a sleepy farming community on the banks of Neshannock Creek into a town of specialty shops. The catalyst for change was the conversion of the old 1810 gristmill into a craft and antique shop in 1984. It wasn't long before other historic buildings became galleries, clothing shops, and cafes. A carriage house was transformed into the Wooden Horse, a store specializing in restored carousel horses and handcrafted wood; a blacksmith shop changed into the Volant Brass & Iron gift shop; and the volunteer fire station assumed new life as Neshannock Creek Outfitters, clothiers. A popular destination for 300 to 400 busloads of visitors a year, the town can become downright congested, but if you're a dedicated shopper, it's worth coping with the crowds.

When lunchtime rolls around, head out to Grove City, where Broadstreet Books & Cafe employs that most felicitous combination—good food and good books. The self-service cafe is to the rear of the first floor of the bookstore, and daily luncheon and dinner specials include items such as hearty navy bean soup and home-style chicken salad. There is an espresso bar, and desserts range from white chocolate coconut torte to lemon meringue pie. The cafe lives up to its motto: "For those with an appetite for reading."

Grove City's history dates from 1798, when a gristmill was established on the banks of Wolf Creek. As home of Grove City College and high-tech industries such as General Electric and Cooper Energies, the city has become one of the fastest growing communities in Mercer County. The downtown boasts a fine collection of shops and stores, but a large percentage of out-of-town visitors head to Wendell August Forge. Billed as the largest and oldest hand-working forge in the country, Wendell August produces forged aluminum, pewter, bronze, and sterling silver giftware entirely by hand using no production machinery. The showroom and museum contain a collection of original items tracing the history of the forge since its beginning in Brockway in 1923, and a self-guided tour of the facility illustrates how forge artisans carry a piece from design to finished product.

Leaving Grove City, you travel on to Slippery Rock, best known for its branch of Pennsylvania State University and for the Applebutter Inn, one of the Commonwealth's finest hostelries. The original structure was built by Michael Christley in 1844 from bricks formed and fired on the premises. Gary and Sandra McKnight purchased the property and in 1987 transformed what was for a time an untenanted derelict into an elegant inn surrounded by perfectly landscaped grounds. Restored woodwork, exposed brick fireplaces, and original chestnut and poplar flooring serve as a backdrop for fine country antiques. The adjacent Wolf Creek School Cafe was moved by the McKnights from a site west of town, and they have incorporated the atmosphere of a one-room 1899 schoolhouse into a fine restaurant serving hearty country breakfasts, unhurried lunches, and prepared-to-order gourmet dinners.

Just south of Slippery Rock and Stone House, Jennings Environmental Education Center's 295 acres provide a small glimpse of genuine prairie in the East. Founded in the late 1950s by the Western Pennsylvania Conservancy to protect and conserve the rare blazing star and the Massasauga rattlesnake, the center is currently under the auspices of the state park system. Late summer and early fall are optimum times to hike the well-maintained trails and enjoy the spiky blooms of the blazing star and other prairie plants. Don't be concerned about coming across a rattler. They are extremely reclusive, and chances of encountering one are minimal.

Passing along the shore of Moraine State Park's Lake Arthur, your view to the west is somewhat limited by dense woodlands. It is hard to believe that this sylvan scene was once heavily scarred and pitted with coal mines, coal strippings, and gas and oil wells. Reclaimed and regenerated, the land now provides recreation in the form of fishing, boating, swimming, hiking, and bicycling along a seven-mile north-shore path. For a good overview of the lake created by the damming of Muddy Creek, take the first left after the State 258 bridge. You will find a boat launch, an old brick Baptist church, and a broad vista of the eastern end of the 3,225-acre lake.

After joining US 422 at the lake's southernmost point, you pass the Pleasant Valley day use area with its boat rental, picnic areas, and swimming beach. Crossing another arm of the lake, you continue west to McConnells Mill State Park in the deep gorge of Slippery Rock Creek. The spectacular 400-foot chasm was cut by a receding ice dam from the Wisconsin ice sheet tens of thousands of years ago. The precipitous terrain, rushing whitewater, deep pools, and smooth water-washed rocks are attraction enough, but the restored gristmill adds a human dimension to the park. Rebuilt by Daniel Kennedy in 1868 after the original was destroyed by fire, the mill was purchased in 1875 by Thomas McConnell and converted into a rolling mill, one of the first in the country. In operation until 1928, when advanced technology made it obsolete, the mill building and surrounding property were conveyed to the Western Pennsylvania Conservancy and later to the state. A tour of the old mill and a walk along wild-flower-dotted trails is an hour or two well spent.

South along old Perry Highway, Connoquenessing Creek winds around the village of Harmony and borders Zelienople on the north and northwest. The towns, so close in proximity, were established by two German immigrants with contrasting life-styles: one an educated aristocrat and the other a leader of a peasant group seeking religious freedom in the New World.

In 1802 Baron Dettmar Friedrich Basse bought 10,000 acres of fertile land, engineered a planned community, and named the town Zelienople after his eldest daughter, Zelie, who arrived in 1807 with her husband, Phillip Passavant.

At about the same time, Johann George Rapp, leader of a German Pietist group, came to America, where in 1804 he purchased 4,000 acres from Basse. He and his followers were known as the "Harmonie Society," a Christian communal congregation of nearly 800 farmers and craftsmen. Basing their life-style on the early Christian Church, they adopted celibacy in 1807 in order to prepare themselves for what they believed to be Christ's second coming and the ensuing millennium. Everyone worked for the good of the society and, in turn, received what they needed to sustain themselves comfortably. After the needs of the community were met, the talents of the people were available to the general public.

Harmonists were successful manufacturers as well as farmers, being known both for their fine wines and, in later years, as makers of cotton and woolen products. They also developed a means of producing high-quality silk, which was awarded top prizes in competitions in New York, Boston, and Philadelphia.

For ten years the society prospered, clearing more than 200 acres of land, building fifty log houses, planting crops, and constructing a number of buildings, many of which still stand. In 1815 the society relocated to Indiana, where they stayed for ten years before returning to Pennsylvania to build Old Economy on the banks of the Ohio in present-day Ambridge.

Zelienople also prospered as a commercial hub and later as an industrial center when Basse discovered iron ore on the land and built one of the first charcoal blast furnaces in western Pennsylvania.

Today's towns are an interesting contrast. Harmony, which was largely resettled by Mennonites after the departure of the Harmonists, is a quiet village, more attuned to the past. Laid out around the Diamond, the old buildings seem suspended in time. The Harmony Museum, adjacent to the Diamond, holds relics of the Harmonist Society and the Mennonites, and a collection of Native American artifacts. Crowning the museum's entranceway is a rendition of the Virgin Sophia, Harmonist symbol of wisdom hand-carved by Frederick Rapp, adopted son of George Rapp and business manager of the society. Below the museum the great arched wine cellar reminds us of the Harmonists' role as early vintners.

Other old buildings have been adapted to modern use. The original brick Harmonist meetinghouse is now part of Grace Church. Several other structures house antique shops, such as the Harmonite Stohr Antiques, with a collection of primitives, limited-edition books, and glassware. The store's massive stone-arched wine cellar is twin to that of the museum. The 1856 Austin Pierce House, built for the first president of the Pittsburgh and Western Railroad, is now the Historic Harmony Inn, which specializes in a variety of ethnic cuisines.

Neighboring Zelienople is a modern, bustling commercial center, which takes pride in its past without losing its momentum toward the future. The Zelienople Historical Society has succeeded in preserving some of the city's history through the acquisition of two historic buildings, the Passavant and Buhl houses.

The Passavant House was first occupied by Zelie Basse Passavant, for whom the town was named, and her husband, Phillip. The home, which is on the National Register, has a composite collection relating to the Passavant family and to the borough. Included in the melange are Zelie's wedding gown, family portraits, and items from the first Passavant store.

The Buhl House, a few doors down from the museum, was constructed in 1805 by Christian Buhl, the town hatter and furrier. It is Zelienople's oldest building and is in the process of being turned into a museum specifically addressing village history.

If you're in town for lunch or dinner, stop at the Kaufman House, a venerable Main Street restaurant, in business since 1903. Ken and Marge Polarski specialize in basic, uncomplicated fare such as prime rib and seafood, and the service is small-town friendly.

For overnight accommodations, there's the Marriott Fairfield Inn in nearby Mars, or if you prefer something more intimate, contact Margo Hogan at Historic Benvenue Manor Bed & Breakfast. Built in 1816 by a family of French aristocrats, the stately manor house sits atop a hill overlooking the town. The five bedrooms, decorated in Victorian style, have stunning views of the surrounding countryside, and Margo is both a gracious hostess and an impressive breakfast cook. All

Old Economy

rolls, muffins, jams, and jellies are homemade; if you prefer, she'll serve you breakfast in bed.

The road from Zelienople to Ambridge winds through western Pennsylvania's hills and hollows, portions paralleling I-80 and other sections roller coasting over two-lane byways. As you approach Ambridge, the rural landscape turns urban. Named for The American Bridge Company at the turn of the century, and formerly the site of its corporate offices and fabricating plant, the borough is a densely settled blue-collar town.

In a six-acre plot set apart, Old Economy Village preserves the social, religious, and economic hub of the Harmony Society. The seventeen restored Harmonist buildings, graceful walks, and well-tended gardens transport you back to 1824, when the society returned to Beaver County from Indiana and built "Oekonomie" on the banks of the Ohio River. Here they prospered until a series of events brought their gradual decline: the departure of one third of the group under the leadership of Count de Leon, a self-styled rival prophet, and, finally, the death of Father Rapp himself in 1847.

The village of Economy was much larger than the present museum grounds, which contain only the business and cultural center of the community. You can get your bearings by obtaining a printed walking tour in the Feast Hall or registering for the hour-and-a-half guided tour with costumed docent. The circuit consists of a slide presentation and a visit to twelve buildings, including George Rapp's elegantly appointed home; the general store; the blacksmith shop; the vaulted wine cellar, where the Harmonists stored their famous vintages; and the Baker House, home to storekeeper Romelius Baker, who headed the society following Rapp's death.

Even if your time is short, take the opportunity to walk in the gardens and reflect on the enterprise that produced such a perfectly ordered setting. Don't miss the pavilion with its pool and graceful statue and the many old varieties of flowers and trees. The harmony of nature reflects the harmony of principle that made these early settlers so instrumental in the development of this part of Pennsylvania.

In the Area

All numbers are within area code 412.

New Wilmington Grange Hall, New Wilmington, 652-1271 or 924-2836.

The Tavern, New Wilmington, 946-2020. Closed Tuesday. Reservations preferred.

Feed Mill Tea Room, New Wilmington, 946-8878. Closed Sunday and Monday.

Behm's Bed & Breakfast, New Wilmington, 946-8641.

The Apple Castle, New Wilmington, 652-3221. Closed Sunday.

Patrick Henry Antiques & Collectibles, New Wilmington, 946-3235. Daily. Sunday by chance.

Volant Mill, Volant, 533-5611.

Wooden Horse Collectibles, Volant, 533-3435.

Volant Brass & Iron, Volant, 533-3322.

Neshannock Creek Outfitters, Volant, 533-2311.

Broadstreet Books & Cafe, Grove City, 458-6763. Closed Sunday.

Wendell August Forge, Grove City, 458-8360. Showroom/museum daily; tours Monday through Friday.

Applebutter Inn and Wolf Creek School Cafe, Slippery Rock, 794-1844.

Jennings Environmental Education Center, Slippery Rock, 794-6011.

Moraine State Park, Portersville, 368-8811.

McConnells Mill State Park, Portersville, 368-8091 or 368-8811.

The Harmony Museum, Harmony, 452-7341. Tuesday through Sunday afternoons from June 1 through October 1; winter by appointment.

Harmonite Stohr & Harmonite Stohr Antiques, Harmony, 452-4616. Closed Monday.

Historic Harmony Inn, Harmony, 452-5124.

The Passavant and Buhl House museums, Zelienople Historical Society, Zelienople, 452-9457. Wednesday and Saturday afternoons from May through September; other times by appointment.

The Kaufman House, Zelienople, 452-8900.

The Marriott Fairfield Inn, Mars, 772-0600.

Historic Benvenue Manor Bed & Breakfast, Zelienople, 452-1710.

Old Economy Village, Ambridge, 266-4500. Closed Mondays and major holidays. Fee.

Lawrence County Tourist Promotion Agency, New Castle (New Wilmington, Volant, and McConnells Mill State Park), 654-5593.

Mercer County Tourist Agency, Sharon (Grove City), 800-637-2370 or 981-5880.

The Magic Forests of West Central Pennsylvania Tourism & Travel Bureau, Brookville (Slippery Rock, Moraine State Park, Harmony, and Zelienople), 800-348-9393 or 814-849-5197.

Beaver County Tourist Promotion Agency, Monaca (Ambridge), 800-342-8192 or 728-0212.

12 ~

Land of

Lakes

Getting there: Take I-90 to exit 11 to State 89.

Highlights: *Give yourself a weekend to explore Pennsylvania's northwest. In and around the town of North East, Lake Erie's fertile shore is blanketed with miles of vineyards and dotted with wineries. The city of Erie dips its toes into the water at Presque Isle's miles of beach. Relive history where Perry's historic flagship, the U.S. Brig Niagara, rides at anchor. Visit the historic Baldwin Reynolds House in Meadville, Conneaut Lake, and the vast Pymatuning Reservoir. The last stop is Greenville, on the route of the old Erie Extension Canal.*

The Route

In Pennsylvania, I-90 runs parallel to the shore of Lake Erie, bridging the gap between New York and Ohio.

To begin your tour, take exit 11 east of Erie and follow State 89 north to North East and the junction of State 5, which runs southwest along the lake shore. Alternate State 5, which begins just east of Erie, accesses the heart of the city.

To reach Presque Isle, turn north on State 832 and enter park lands. Return south on State 832 to US 20 east and I-79 south. Take exit 41 to Interstate Road and State 99 south through Edinboro. Joining US 6/19 south, you arrive in Meadville and pick up US 6/322 west to Conneaut Lake. At the southern point of the lake, take State 18 north to Harmonsburg, where you follow the Harmonsburg Road west to US 6. In Linesville, turn south on SR 3011 and right on SR 3005 to Jamestown. Take State 58 south to Greenville, and return to I-79 at Clarks Mills via State 358 east. The approximate total miles is 121.

Go to North East in the fall, when the vineyards are golden garlands and the crisp air and bright sunshine bring the grapes to sweet perfection. Huge automated pickers rattle and clank down rows of Niagaras, Chardonnays, and Pinot Noirs; and mammoth open-bed trucks filled with Concords hurry to the Welch plant for processing into juice, jellies, and jams. Little did William Griffith dream when he planted three acres of grapes in the early 1850s that North East would become one of the largest Concord grape–growing regions in the world.

A charming Victorian town listed on the National Register, North East takes its name from its position in the county, not the state. Radiating out from Gibson Park, with its arching trees and modest turn-of-the-century fountain, the graceful streets seem designed for leisurely strolls. For a brochure detailing a walking tour of historic homes, check with the Chamber of Commerce office on East Main. They can also provide an area map in case you want to wander the back roads or locate a roadside stand for fresh cider, a bushel of tart Granny Smiths, or a basket of Concords.

If it's fall, one operation you don't want to miss is Mums by Paschke on East Main. What began as D. C. Paschke's hobby has grown to a business that draws visitors from all points of the compass. Jack Paschke and his son Ken continue the family tradition with what has to be one of the biggest chrysanthemum displays in the country. Acres and acres of

Gibson Park at the center of North East

multicolored blossoms stretch ribbons of color through the surrounding fields, and in the display building Paschke sells more than 1,200 plants in 150 varieties to eager buyers.

Of course, when you're in grape country, you visit the wineries. Mazza Vineyards, Penn Shore Winery, and Heritage Wine Cellars all offer tastings and take neophytes through the wine-making process.

Rail fans will find the Lake Shore Railway Museum worth a stop. The former New York Central passenger depot is staffed with good-natured volunteers who are happy to share their knowledge of the area's rail history and point out prized collections, such as the Centralized Traffic Control Board, which shows how a single dispatcher can control many large stretches of track at a time.

Brown's Village Inn is a good base of operations while in North East. Rebecca Brown is a gracious hostess who welcomes guests at her Federal-style 1832 home, which once served as a stagecoach tavern and station for the underground railroad. The spacious rooms are antique furnished, and the breakfasts sumptuous.

East Lake Road leads west to Erie through a patchwork landscape of orchards and vineyards. Although the city of Erie is Pennsylvania's third largest, it has a small-town feel. Its waterfront, where giant Great Lakes' freighters were once built, worked, and wintered, is undergoing a rebirth as a recreational area. The downtown Bayfront District is home to the city's major arts organizations. The Erie Art Museum in the Greek Revival Old Customs House has a variety of changing exhibits in its main galleries, but its greatest fascination is "The Avalon Restaurant," by Lisa Lichtenfels. The permanent installation depicts in one-third life-size soft sculpture a moment in the life of a now-defunct Erie diner. The detail is impressive, and the characterizations are hilarious. Regulars such as Violent Viola and the little Mennonite girl were modeled from real characters. The waitress is an artist self-portrait.

Next to the museum, the Erie County Historical Society maintains the Erie History Center, with displays focusing on local industry and architecture, and the elegant Cashiers House, built in 1839 for the chief executive officer of the Erie Branch of the U.S. Bank of Pennsylvania. It contains furnishings of the period. Both buildings welcome visitors.

Don't leave Erie before visiting the U.S. Brig *Niagara*, the square-rigged, two-masted warship used as a relief flagship by Commodore Oliver Hazard Perry in his defeat of the British Lake Erie fleet on September 10, 1813. On board after the battle, Perry penned his now-classic victory message, "We have met the enemy, and they are ours."

This last surviving relic of the War of 1812 is berthed at the foot of Holland Street and serves as the centerpiece of a maritime museum, which is expected to open in spring 1995. Reconstructed in 1989 by the state Historical and Museum Commission, the vessel is completely seaworthy and now serves as flagship of the Commonwealth of Pennsylvania. In port it's a living history repository of naval history.

While downtown, you might want to do a little shopping and catch a meal. The Glass Growers Gallery at Seventh and Holland has one of the finest collections of handmade crafts in northwestern Pennsylvania. Located in a restored nineteenth-century church, it carries everything from handwoven goods to kaleidoscopes.

The Rotunda of Union Station Center is an elegant eatery located in the restored Art Deco railroad station. The high ceiling Rotunda and Concourse rooms, with imported Italian marble and brass-gridded terrazzo floors, earned the building the nickname "The Taj Majal" of Erie when it was built in the 1920s. The food is 100 percent American, with steaks, seafood, and pastas predominating, and in the Depot Lounge a bounteous free buffet is served from 5:00 P. M. to 7:00 P.M. on weekdays. The hand-carved roast beef sandwiches on Thursday are especially tasty.

To the west of the city and almost encircling it in a protective arm, the peninsula of Presque Isle encloses the bay and provides a nonpareil recreation area. The 3,200-acre state park juts seven miles into the lake and is rimmed with swimming beaches and laced with hiking trails. The terrain is diverse, with a sand and water lakeshore environment changing to a climax forest within two miles. The wooded areas and plentiful ponds offer refuge to the many spring and fall migrating birds; more than 300 different species have been identified here. Although a fourteen-mile scenic roadway loops through the park, past the lighthouse, Coast Guard station, and the monument to Perry, most folks enjoy getting out for a stroll on one of the several walkways, such as the Sidewalk Trail through the marshy ecological reservation.

Heading south, you wind along the Appalachian Plateau, a rural landscape threaded with shallow stream valleys. At the intersection of State 99 and US 6N in Edinboro, the Crossroads Dinor [sic] dispenses daily specials, including homemade soups and chicken and biscuits. Originally, the town landmark was a trolley car hauling coal to Edinboro Normal School and transporting milk back to Erie. No one knows how the eatery got its unusual name, but everyone knows it's the place to stop for a cup of java and a piece of pie.

In Cambridge Springs the Riverside Inn stands in faded gentility on the banks of French Creek. A Victorian-era mineral spa resurrected as a hotel and summer dinner theater, it has a good kitchen, proper turn-of-the-century public rooms, and unpretentious accommodations.

Meadville is the hub of Crawford County; it is an attractive, bustling town centered around Diamond Park, with memorials, statues, fountain, and gazebo. It's a given that every citizen of Meadville passes the oval-shaped Diamond at least once a day.

The Baldwin-Reynolds House on Terrace Street overlooks the former channel of French Creek and the old Indian route, the Venango Path. A National Register property, the four-story Federal-style mansion was built between 1842 and 1843 by Henry Baldwin, a Meadville lawyer and later a Pittsburgh iron furnace owner. He was three times elected to the U.S. House of Representatives and served on the U.S. Supreme Court from 1830 until his death in 1844.

Patterned after a Tennessee home that Baldwin admired, the mansion has twenty-five rooms of antique furnishings and displays. Especially noteworthy are the parquet floors, black walnut woodwork, the library with its secret panels on the first floor and on the second floor, the curly maple wood-work in two bedrooms. On the three-acre parklike grounds, a country doctor's office provides a glimpse into the life of a nineteenth-century physician.

If you love farmers' markets, don't miss the Market House, built in 1870 and in continuous use since then. You'll meet people such as Claire Wiant, who sets up on the old brick building's shaded porch. She's sold produce from her 137-acre East Meadville Township farm for thirty years at the same site.

The market's first-floor interior is chockablock with stalls selling everything from firm ripe tomatoes to sticky buns. At the entrance, Sally Custard has set up her tidy little restaurant, the Feed Mill. She opens at 6:00 a.m. to catch hungry early market-goers and closes at 3:00 P.M. Breakfast is generous and very reasonable. Lunch is sandwiches, homemade soup (she makes it in twenty-gallon batches), and hot open-faced sandwiches with potatoes and gravy. The meat loaf is a real winner.

If you're after something a tad fancier, Sarah Maher runs Sarah's Place on Chestnut Street. A gourmet cook with a

The Market House at Meadville

reputation for innovation, Sarah's dinners run to specialties such as chicken with summer berries or sauté of scallops in garlic and herbs. Lunches feature German vegetable soup, salads, elaborate sandwiches, and her own Cincinnati chili.

Meadville's newest draw is the reopened and revamped Academy Theatre, built in 1885 by Earnest Hempstead and presented to the people of Meadville as a performance house, concert hall, and community gathering place. The 1920s saw its transformation into a movie theater, and the next decades weren't kind. In 1988 the Meadville Redevelopment Authority came to its rescue, purchased the building, renovated it, and opened it as a year-round performing arts center staging plays, musicals, children's theater, film festivals, and works by the local community theater.

Leaving Meadville, you skirt the shore of Conneaut Lake and head west to Linesville on the Pymatuning Reservoir. Once a great marshy wetland inhabited by prehistoric "mound builders," the lake was created in 1931 for flood control and to regulate the flow of water in the Shenango and Beaver rivers. The sickle-shaped, sixteen-mile-long lake with seventy miles of shoreline rides the Ohio/Pennsylvania border and is home to nesting bald eagles, herons, osprey, ducks, geese, and other waterfowl. A wildlife refuge of 2,500 acres of water and 1,170 acres of land, the area furnishes the birds a protected location during fall and spring migrations.

After the village of Linesville, your first stop is the Linesville Fish Culture Station, where the Pennsylvania Fish Commission raises walleye, Coho salmon, black crappie, yellow perch, and muskies for release in the Pymatuning and other Commonwealth waters. The hatchery building has a variety of exhibits, including a silo-type aquarium with all the species found in the reservoir. On the grounds hatchlings of all shapes and sizes fill the concrete pens with flashes of silver scales.

The Pymatuning Wildlife Management Area Visitor Center is located on Ford Island, between the hatchery and the spillway. The museum displays nearly 300 mounted wildlife specimens, exhibits, and wildlife dioramas. If stuffed birds aren't to your liking, take a walk on the short, well-defined nature trail or try to catch a glimpse of the nesting eagles through the pay binoculars on the terrace.

Everyone reacts differently to the spillway, where "ducks walk on fishes' backs." It's definitely a curiosity. Where the waters of the lake exit through an opening in the dam wall, thousands of carp gather to be fed scraps of bread, which visitors either bring or buy at a small on-site stand. The greedy fish are matched by equally greedy mallard ducks, and the competition is so intense that the ducks slip, slide, and slither over the fishes' backs.

As you head south through Pennsylvania's lakeland, stop in Jamestown at Victoria's Cafe in historic Mark Twain Manor. Whether or not the stately 1855 brick home is truly haunted by a bride killed on the way to her wedding, and by a small black child in Civil War dress, the food is good and the atmosphere inviting, not eldritch.

Greenville is a surprising little town with four-year Thiel College, a symphony orchestra, and two museums that would be the envy of a larger village. The Canal Museum illustrates the history of the Erie Extension Canal, complete with a full-size replica of an original canal boat, the forty-foot *Rufus S. Reed*. There's even a potbellied stove in the crew's quarters. Other exhibits include a diorama of a section of the canal, historic posters, and a working model of a canal lock.

The Greenville Railroad Museum boasts a variety of rolling stock, including the only remaining example of the massive 322-ton switch locomotives built for the Union Railroad in 1936 at the Philadelphia Baldwin Locomotive Works.

Engine 604 features a unique 0-10-2 wheel alignment and is displayed with a coal tender, hopper car, and caboose.

In the station museum, there is an "Empire" touring car, manufactured in 1913–1914 by Greenville Metal Products, and a prototype of the first parachute, invented by Stefan Banic, a Slovak immigrant who worked in the coal mines near Greenville. This bizarre early model consisted of an umbrella-like device that the wearer wore strapped to his chest and secured with a hip harness.

Tom and Diane Ochs have a cozy 100-year-old Victorian Queen Anne B & B on what was once the local Merchants' Row and now, more modestly, just Eagle Street. The four bedrooms in the Phillips 1890 House are decorated in country antiques; the Toy Room, with its collection of old-fashioned children's playthings, is especially winsome.

Before you leave the area, you might want to take State 18 three miles out of town to the Brucker Great Blue Heron Sanctuary of Thiel College, the largest collection of breeding great blues in Pennsylvania. Late winter and spring are the best times to see the birds before foliage obscures the view. Although walking in the sanctuary is prohibited during nesting, an observation shelter is open year-round.

In the Area

All numbers are within area code 814 unless otherwise indicated.

North East Chamber of Commerce, North East, 725-4262.

Mums by Paschke, North East, 725-9860. Daily in September and October.

Mazza Vineyards, North East, 725-8695.

Penn Shore Winery, North East, 725-8688.

Heritage Wine Cellars, North East, 725-8015.

Lake Shore Railway Museum, North East, 825-2724.
Wednesday through Sunday from Memorial Day
through Labor Day; Saturday and Sunday in
September.

Brown's Village Inn, North East, 725-5522.

Erie Art Museum, Erie, 459-5477. Closed Monday.

Erie History Center, Erie, 454-1813. Tuesday through
Saturday. Tours of the Cashiers House, Tuesday
through Saturday afternoons.

U.S. Brig *Niagara*, Erie, 871-4596 or 452-BRIG. Daily from
Memorial Day through Labor Day; Saturday and
Sunday from April through Memorial Day weekend
and after Labor Day week through October 31; closed
November through March. Fee.

Glass Growers Gallery, Erie, 453-3758.

The Rotunda of Union Station Center, Erie, 453-4000.

Presque Isle State Park, Erie, 871-4251.

Crossroads Dinor, Edinboro, 734-1912. Closed Monday.

The Riverside Inn, Cambridge Springs, 800-964-5173.

The Baldwin-Reynolds House Museum, Meadville,
724-6080. Wednesday, Saturday, and Sunday afternoons
from Memorial Day through Labor Day. Fee.

Market House, Meadville, 337-8023 or 336-2056. Tuesday
through Saturday.

Sarah's Place, Meadville, 333-8914. Closed Sunday and
Monday.

The Academy Theatre, Meadville, 337-8000.

Pennsylvania Fish Commission Linesville Hatchery,
Linesville, 437-5774.

Pymatuning Wildlife Management Area Visitor Center,
Linesville, 683-5545.

Pymatuning State Park, Jamestown, 412-932-3141.

Mark Twain Manor, Jamestown, 412-932-5455 or 588-7778.

The Canal Museum, Greenville, 412-588-7540. Thursday through Sunday afternoons from Memorial Day through Labor Day; Saturday and Sunday afternoons from Labor Day through December 31. Fee.

Greenville Railroad Museum, Greenville, 412-588-4009, or Greenville Area Chamber of Commerce, 588-7150.

Phillips 1890 House, Greenville, 412-588-8887.

Brucker Great Blue Heron Sanctuary of Thiel College, Greenville, 216-448-8911 (Edward Brucker) or 412-588-7700 (Biology Department, Thiel College).

Tourist and Convention Bureau of Erie County, Erie, 454-7191.

Crawford County Tourist Association, Meadville, 800-332-2338 or 333-1258.

Greenville Area Chamber of Commerce, Greenville, 412-588-7150.

13 ~

A Merely Marvelous Winter Weekend

Getting there: Take I-80 to Williamsport, exit 31.

Highlights: *Sharpen the blades on your ice skates, glide-wax your cross-country skis, and pack your courage for a ride on the Eagles Mere ice toboggan run.*

The Route

From I-80 east of the Susquehanna River, take exit 31, Williamsport, to I-180 north. Exit I-180 at Muncy, and follow State 405 north to Hughsville, where it joins US 220 north. At Muncy Valley, take State 42 north to Eagles Mere.

Leaving the village, continue on State 42 north to Laporte, join US 220 north for a brief distance, and turn north on State 154 to Forksville. Pick up State 87 south to I-180, Montoursville, about seven miles east of Williamsport. The approximate total miles is eighty-one.

When the winter doldrums strike and spring seems eons away, it's time to take a weekend and head for Eagles Mere, "the town time forgot." No doctor can prescribe a better cure for the wintertime blues than the challenge of skiing a cross-country run in the woods, tracing a figure eight on the pond, or mounting a sled for a hair-raising quarter-mile-long run down an ice-covered slide.

Eagles Mere is a preserved Victorian microcosm, a part of the past surviving today. Known originally as Lewis Lake and the site of an early glass factory, the mile-long spring-fed loch later attracted the attention of entrepreneurs who built hotels and boardinghouses. The coming of the railroad spurred the growth not only of hotels but also private "cottages" on the scale only Victorians could imagine. Wealthy families came for the summer with servants and nannies, frequenting hotels such as the Crestmont, constructed in 1900 on the hill to the east of the lake. There was golf at the country club, picnics, boating, tennis, and a never-ending round of parties.

Although the grand hotels are gone—the victims of age and economics—Eagles Mere lives on even in winter. There's an assortment of cross-country ski runs and ice skating on the outlet pond, but the star of the seasonal show is the famous toboggan run. Every year in mid-January and February when the ice on the lake reaches a thickness of a foot or more, the fire company follows a ritual initiated in 1903. Lake Street, the long hill leading down to the water, is cordoned off, and volunteers begin the task of building the ice ramp for the run. Using tools of another era, they cut 900 blocks of ice from the lake, each 44 by 15.5 inches and weighing 250 pounds. These are moved laboriously into position side by side down the road and onto the lake. Using a special device, two grooves are cut in the ice to channel the sled, which has runners and is specially designed for the purpose. Sleds are rented on an hourly basis. To keep you warm while you wait your turn, there's a Snack Shack serving cocoa, coffee, brownies, hot dogs, and the like.

Down the toboggan run at Eagles Mere

You never forget your first ride on the toboggan. The start of the run is deceptively sedate, but shortly the road dips, and the toboggan accelerates. Soon you are screaming down the slope, runners chattering in their grooves and clattering over the joints in the ice. The wind lashes your hair and your eyes tear. The trees lining the road turn to a black blur, and the hard blue ice of the lake rises up to meet you. It's all over in less than a minute; then it's hike up the hill and do it all over again. How fast do you go? Rumor has it that speeds up to 60 mph are reached, but a lot depends on conditions and the combined weight of the sled occupants.

With an elevation of more than 2,000 feet, Eagles Mere and the surrounding communities frequently have snow cover when city backyards are bare. This felicitous situation combined with miles of unspoiled forest make the area a mecca for cross-country skiers. Since 1969 Rip Hanley and his wife, Carolyn, have catered to weekend warriors at Happy Hill Cross Country Ski Area. With fifty kilometers of groomed and set track and additional wilderness trails, Happy Hill brings smiles from everyone from expert Nordic skiers to beginners. Several of the trails follow the route of the old Eagles Mere narrow gauge railroad, which ran from Sonestown to the village. Other runs trace the contours of the mountain, with climbs up to Chestnut Ridge and some exhilarating downhills back to the road.

Cross-country skiing, as its devotees will tell you, is different in many ways from downhill skiing. Although the skinny skis take a bit of getting used to in the beginning, they are infinitely easier for a novice to control than downhill skis. Lessons help a lot, but a reasonably coordinated person can enjoy short, even treks right from the start. There are no crowds, no lift lines, and no mechanical gadgets yanking you uphill. On bitter cold days, the woods provide shelter, and the force of your exertion keeps you warm. On balmy days, the open meadows and lakeside beckon.

On your way to Eagles Mere, you may have noticed a sign for Crystal Lake Camps off US 220 near the village of Tivoli. If you turn down Highland Lake Road, you will climb steadily for five miles to an elevated plateau, which has some of the finest cross-country trails in Pennsylvania. Joe and Dottie Alford do a yeoman's job of maintaining twenty-five miles of groomed and set track on 960 acres of land encompassing every sort of terrain. There are two lakes, three beaver ponds, miles of woods, and sunny meadows. A boys' camp in summer, Crystal Lake is a decidedly low-key operation attracting both day skiers and overnight groups who put up in the lodges and cottages and eat cafeteria-style in the big mess hall. There are ski rentals and instruction, but most of all, there are the trails—some climbing the ridge with beautiful lake vistas, some tracing the dim hemlock groves that shelter snow even in mild winters. A run around Boardpile and past Whipple Mill cabin will put roses in your cheeks and whip up your appetite for a fine dinner.

On your return to Eagles Mere, stop at Katie's Country Store in Muncy Valley, where Katie Becardi has taken a 1917 general store and converted it into a country variety emporium stocking everything from penny candy to Pennsylvania stoneware. After browsing through the store, walk around back to the building housing Katie's Closet, a women's clothing boutique, and Strawbridge Art Gallery, which specializes in works by local artists, such as Ruth Wilson and David Hopkins.

Back in Eagles Mere, there's a collection of shops clustered around the old mercantile area, just up the street from the town's landmark clock. Shop hours vary widely by season, but you should find several of the specialty emporiums open winter weekends when the slide is operating. In addition to varied handicrafts, Kathleen Deasy's Mere Trifles specializes in unusual and beautiful jewelry. Her display cases glitter with silver and vermeil and semiprecious stones.

Caravan Books lodges in the same building, and they carry two floors of current, discounted, and remaindered books.

Across the lot, Jim and Kay Thomas's Someplace Special stocks a variety of old wall and mantel clocks plus a general line of antiques. At Market Street Connection in the old general store, Becky Bird has filled the cavernous old showroom with Yield House furniture, a selection of accent pieces in the American lodge style, Christmas and holiday decorations, and ready-made house banners (they'll also design to order).

When it comes to accommodations, you have a choice of country inn or bed and breakfast. The Crestmont Inn sits on the town's highest hill, and with its attractive gray siding and white trim, it cleverly conceals its origins as the washhouse of the old Crestmont Hotel, which was demolished in 1981–82. The rooms and suites are tastefully decorated in warm country style, and innkeepers John and Jane Wiley set a fine table, with a selection of entrées ranging from lamb chops in honey mustard sauce to salmon poached in court bouillon with a dollop of sour cream and dill. The dining room is a study in unpretentious refinement, with its pink and white napery and oil paintings by local artists gracing the walls.

Down the hill in town, the Eagles Mere Inn began life as a boardinghouse for the workmen hired to build the hotels and cottages. Over the years the inn has had a reputation for comfortable, if not stylish, rooms and an excellent table. Innkeepers Peter and Susan Glaubitz have only improved on a good thing, with Susan using her decorator's skill in transforming the chambers into inviting bowers and Peter utilizing his years in three- and four-star hotels and restaurants to make sure that the guests have a visit to remember. Dinners are special events that might start off with a cheddar spread laced with pineapple and horseradish and follow with French onion soup, a salad of mixed greens with orange-walnut dressing, Haagen Dazs fruit sorbet with mint, chicken dijon or roast prime rib with horseradish sauce, snap peas and pine nut rice, and finally an assortment of delicious desserts, such as Susan's grandmother's pecan pie with whipped cream, or hummingbird cake. Peter's wine cellar is extensive, as you'd expect from a man who has acted as a judge of an international wine competition and who is an officer in La Confrerie de la Chaine des Rotisseurs.

Pat and Dennis Dougherty are a couple who genuinely enjoy people, and they have converted their 1947 ranch on Allegheny Avenue into Shady Lane Lodge bed and breakfast where the emphasis is on comfort and hospitality. Their location has one of the grandest views in town—miles and miles of forest rising to Chestnut Ridge and North Mountain.

The Flora Villa Inne, a handsome Victorian painted lady next to the town clock, is the town's second bed and breakfast. Built in the 1880s as Eagles Mere's only year-round inn, the Flora Villa has had the dust of time polished off its six rooms and inviting parlors. Innkeepers Jay and Shannon Wilkinson make guests feel like members of the family. Sharing kitchen chores in the morning, they turn out breakfasts to rely on— fresh fruit, juice, and entrées such as cheese strata or buttermilk pancakes.

When you leave Eagles Mere, you follow the Loyalsock River through Wyoming State Forest and World's End State Park. In Forksville, take a minute to drive through the covered bridge to the village. At the general store you can gas up for the trip home, order a pizza or sub, or pick up an order of their excellent Cajun sausage. After you leave Forksville, the Loyalsock Valley stretches miles to the south, widening as the river stretches to reach the Susquehanna near Williamsport.

In the Area

All numbers are within area code 717 unless otherwise indicated.

Eagles Mere Toboggan Slide, Eagles Mere, 525-3244.

Hanley's Happy Hill Cross Country Ski Area, Eagles Mere, 525-3461.

Crystal Lake Camps, Hughesville, 584-2698.

Katies Country Store/Strawbridge Art Gallery/Katie's Closet, Muncy Valley, 482-2911. Daily from May through December; Saturday and Sunday from January through April.

Eagles Mere Village Shoppes, Eagles Mere Village, Inc., 525-3503. Irregular hours: Weekends only from January through June and from September through December; Wednesday through Sunday in July and August.

Crestmont Inn, Eagles Mere, 525-3519.

Eagles Mere Inn, Eagles Mere, 800-426-3273 in OH, WV, VA, MD, DE, NJ, NY, CT, PA. 525-3273. Dining by reservation. Chili and pizza in pub when slide operating.

Shady Lane Lodge, Eagles Mere, 525-3394.

Flora Villa Inne, Eagles Mere, 525-3245.

Forksville General Store, Forksville, 924-4982.

Endless Mountains Visitors Bureau, Tunkhannock, 836-5431.

14 ~

Far from the Madding Crowds

Getting there: Take I-81 to Lenox, exit 64 to State 106 east and State 374 east.

Highlights: *Go cross-country skiing through a snow-stilled forest with no other company but your thoughts and the scold of the chickadees. Ski a downhill area with one of Pennsylvania's greatest verticals and never stand in a lift line or fight for the last seat in the base lodge cafeteria.*

The Route

From I-81 north of Scranton, take Lenox exit 64 and follow State 106 east and State 374 east to Elk Mountain.

Leaving Elk, rejoin State 374 east. Turn north on State 171 and east on State 370 to Starlight. From Starlight, stay on State 370 east to State 191 north, and join State 17 in Hancock, New York. The approximate total miles is thirty-six.

If you're a skier, you love the winter, love the frosty cold and the silent world the snow brings. What you don't love are

crowds—all those noisy, pushy, polluting crowds you en-
counter at too many ski resorts. If you believe that this is the
price you pay for your sport, take heart. In Pennsylvania's
Endless Mountains, you will rediscover what made you fall in
love with winter in the first place.

North of Scranton, the Endless Mountains stretch across
a block of four counties, with New York state to the north and
the Pocono Mountains to the east. If you've ever taken US 6,
the Grand Army of the Republic Highway, from east to west,
you have traversed this land of hill set upon hill, a dimpled
landscape of forested knolls and creek-fed lakes dotted only
occasionally with small towns.

When you leave I-81, you head into this vast preserve. If
it's Friday night and the work week is just an hour or two
behind you, stop at Bingham's Restaurant in Lenox for dinner. The service is friendly and the food is pure home-style.
You can get entrées ranging from broiled salmon to roast pork
loin, or if you're feeling daring, try the buffalo chop steak. The
specials change every night, and the dessert selection always
includes at least ten home-baked pies.

From the restaurant it's only 3.5 miles to your bed and
breakfast, Wiffy Bog Farm. Jim and Valerie Cole will give you
a warm welcome to their 100-year-old Victorian, even on the
coldest night, and you'll enjoy a peaceful rest tucked under
the covers in one of their seven guest rooms, two suites,
or two-bedroom apartments with kitchen facilities. The
rooms are all individually decorated in country antiques
and family heirlooms. The downstairs is so appealing that
guests tend to put off bedtime—congregating in the living
room by the woodstove, playing pool in the game room, or
singing around the grand piano in the music room. Skiers
with sore muscles will be found basking in the liquid warmth
of the hot tub. If the weather has been good and the ice on
the pond is thick, a couple of hardy souls may be skating by
moonlight.

Wiffy Bog Farm in the Endless Mountains

The next morning you'll pull out your parka and long johns and get ready for a day at Elk Mountain. Before you leave, Valerie will be sure you have a good day's foundation with a bounteous country breakfast.

Elk Mountain is just five miles from the farm, and after Blue Knob near Altoona, it has the greatest vertical drop in the state. If Mother Nature has been stingy with those hexagonal flakes, you need not worry; Pennsylvania ski area operators know how to generate snow in almost any weather. All they need is temperatures below freezing, and those snowmaking machines roar into action.

Whether tyro or adept, there is a trail to suit your abilities. Beginners have their own ballroom area at the base and a carefully tended double chair. Graduates from this area can move over to the more challenging Middle Chair, which services East and West Slopes.

146

Expert skiers play on nine trails ranging from show-off Susquehanna to moguled Tunkhannock; mere mortals enjoy a selection of cruising trails such as classic Delaware. With its 1,000-foot vertical, a good consistent pitch, and top to bottom skiing with every run, Elk gives full value for the price of a day lift ticket.

Like any full-service area, Elk has a ski school headed by professionals, a fully equipped rental shop, and a retail ski shop with everything from that pair of goggles you forgot to the latest in ski fashion. For children, there is the SKI-Wee, a fun-oriented learning program, and a nursery for those too young to hit the slopes. In addition to the cafeteria for quick refueling, there's the WinterGarden restaurants, slopeside for casual dining or the balcony for white-tablecloth service. Balcony windows overlook the mountain, and in the evening with the trails lighted for night skiing, the view is truly magical.

Leaving Elk, you head north into a region of ponds and streams, the prettiest of which might be the miniloch where Jack and Judy McMahon run the Inn at Starlight Lake. This rambling rustic is a favorite for cross-country skiers or couples just wanting to get away from it all for a day or two. The inn dates from 1909 and is a prime example of a turn-of-the-century resort, with commodious common rooms, a sweeping porch, and lakeside cottages. The main house has fourteen rooms, all decorated in nonfussy country style; the Annex House with its three bedrooms is perfect for families and groups. The remaining nine rooms are scattered through three cottages and include a suite with double jacuzzi.

A hearty country breakfast starts the day with freshly squeezed juice, newly brewed coffee, and a selection of home-baked rolls and muffins. Don't pass up the three-flour pancakes with blueberry topping, yeast waffles with maple syrup, or French toast made with brioche dough. You'll burn those calories in a day of skiing.

Well fortified, you're ready to strap on those skis and take a cross-country jaunt over the inn's ten miles of groomed and tracked trails. Rentals and lessons are available from the ski school. There's a variety of terrain, from a "bunny hill" to "Yes, You Can," which speaks for itself. One of the most pleasant runs is the route around the lake, which provides beautiful views and easy going.

After lunch on the inn porch, you may be up to another trek or you may elect to sit in the lodge and warm your toes next to the fireplace. Perhaps you'll try your luck at Scrabble in the game room or just ease back in a chair with a good book.

When the indigo veil of evening steals across the lake, skiers and loafers alike gather to trade stories of the day's activities and anticipate dinner with winter-sharpened appetites. Entrées may include a crisp roast duckling, tender lamb chops with artichokes, or fresh fish. There's always homemade pasta prepared in a variety of ways, and vegetarians will delight to crêpes and black beans with a sauce of roasted red peppers and almonds. The inn makes all its own ice cream and sherbets, and of course there's pie and cake.

After a full meal, eyelids get heavy, but most guests manage to stay awake through the old-time movies before heading for the comforts of bed. Morning will arrive quickly, and there are new trails to be explored.

In the Area

All numbers are within area code 717 unless otherwise indicated.

Bingham's Family Restaurant, Lenox, 222-9666.

Wiffy Bog Farm Bed & Breakfast, Uniondale, 222-9865.

Elk Mountain Ski Resort, Uniondale, 679-2611. Snow
    reports, 800-233-4131.

The Inn at Starlight Lake, Starlight, 800-248-2519 or 798-2519.

Endless Mountains Visitors Bureau, Tunkhannock, 836-5431.

Pocono Mountains Vacation Bureau, Stroudsburg, 424-6050
    or 800-762-6667.

Index

Index

Index

RESTAURANTS, BAKERIES,
CAFES and the DINOR
(*cont.*)
WinterGarden, Uniondale, 147
Wolf Creek School Cafe,
Slippery Rock, 114–115
Woodloch Pines bakeshop,
Hawley, 8

SCHOOLS. *See* COLLEGES,
SCHOOLS and
UNIVERSITIES
SHOPS. *See* CRAFT and GIFT
SHOPS
SPECIAL EVENTS. *See*
THEATERS and SPECIAL
EVENTS
STATUES. *See* CEMETERIES,
STATUES and TOWERS

THEATERS and SPECIAL
EVENTS
Academy Theatre, Meadville,
131
Allenberry Resort Inn and
Playhouse, Boiling Springs, 58
Antique Market, New Oxford,
61
Bark Peelers' Convention,
Galeton, 97
Blue Mountain & Reading
Railroad, South Hamburg,
36–38
Carlisle Fairgrounds, 55
Dorflinger-Suydam Wildlife
Sanctuary, White Mills, 9
FolkFest, Johnstown, 108
Fort Ligonier, Ligonier, 83–84
Laurel Festival, Wellsboro, 96
A. Lincoln's Place Theatre,
Gettysburg, 61
National Cemetery, Gettysburg,
59–61

Quilt auction, New
Wilmington, 112
Renninger's Antiques and
Farmers' Market, Kutztown,
34
Shawnee Theatre Summer
Playhouse, Delaware Water
Gap, 4
Washington Crossing Historic
Park, McConkey's Ferry,
25–26
TOWERS. *See* CEMETERIES,
STATUES and TOWERS
TOWNS. *See* CITIES and
TOWNS
TRAVEL and TOURISM
Historic Lancaster Walking
Tour, 45
Presque Isle scenic roadway,
128
River Road, Delaware Water
Gap, 4
Walking tour, Bellefonte, 70
Walking tour, Boiling Springs,
57
Walking tour, North East, 124

UNIVERSITIES. *See* COLLEGES,
SCHOOLS and
UNIVERSITIES

VINEYARDS. *See* FARMS,
FARMERS' MARKETS,
ORCHARDS and
VINEYARDS

WELL-KNOWN PEOPLE
Chief Bender, 54
Daniel Boone, 38
James Buchanan, 45
Christopher Columbus, 74–75
Red Grange, 98

Index

Other titles in the Country Roads series:

Country Roads of Michigan
Country Roads of Massachusetts
Country Roads of Illinois
Country Roads of New Hampshire
Country Roads of Oregon
Country Roads of New York
Country Roads of Indiana
Country Roads of Ohio
Country Roads of Vermont
Country Roads of Washington
Country Roads of Quebec
Country Days in New York City
Country Roads of Kentucky
Country Roads of Hawaii

All books are $9.95 at bookstores.
Or order directly from the publisher (add $3.00
shipping & handling for direct orders):

Country Roads Press
P.O. Box 286
Castine, Maine 04421
Toll-free phone number: **800-729-9179**